I0834800

SATAN'S DEN EXPOSED

SATAN'S DEN EXPOSED

by the

Desert Journal

Bill Johnson
Fred Mramor
David Pierre

About the Cover:
Original art of tortured doll by Josh Bond
www.cynicarts.com
Photograph by David Pierre
Illustration by Bill Johnson

© Copyright 2004, Desert Journal

All rights reserved. No part of this book may be used or reproduced in any manner, stored in a retrieval system, or transmitted by any means, electronic, mechanical, photocopying, recording, or otherwise without written permission from the author except in the case of brief quotations embodied in critical articles or reviews. For information write to Fender Tucker at Ramble House.

Published in the United States of America

Ramble House Paperback First Edition/February 2004

CreateSpace Edition/May 2009

ISBN 13: 978-1-60543-087-4

ISBN 10: 1-60543-087-0

RAMBLE HOUSE
10329 Sheephead Drive
Vancleave MS 39565
www.ramblehouse.com

Dedication

...To the living:

This book is dedicated to the victims, both survivors and the dead, but first our respects to the living, all whose bravery kept them alive and prevented more victims: first, to Cynthia, the last victim to escape the torture chambers—without you, there would have been dozens of more victims; and to Kelly, another survivor whose memory of torment partially became restored and whose credible testimony—along with Cynthia's and Angie's—of one of justice's most incredible, unbelievably sick cases—nailed and sealed shut their tormentors' convictions. You are all heroes. May your hearts be filled with peace and contentment now, the rest of the days of your lives and into eternity…

...To the dead:

I further dedicate this book to those who are not so fortunate to be alive today: first, to our short-time business acquaintance (and I also considered her a friend) Marie Parker—may ALL of your tormentors and ALL of your murderers face the furor of truth and swift justice; secondly, to Angie, who also was a survivor along with Cynthia and Kelly but whose death from pneumonia and heart failure—which came after her entanglement with Sierra County's most evil criminals ever known and during the prosecution of her tormentors—is most unfortunate; and lastly to all of the unknown deceased victims—may you have resolve and peace in your hearts: if truth and justice are blind to these evil acts and evil people here on earth, there is the Judgment Day. May all of them burn in Hell!

And as a testament of my dedication to all of the victims, I vow to keep this book of their trials and tribulations updated with new facts and the truth to ensure that justice will go blind no more…

Bill Johnson
Editor & Publisher of the Desert Journal
– www.desertjournalonline.com
August 16, 2003

Table of Contents

Stories by Headlines:

The Year 1999

The Year 2000

The Year 2001

The Year 2002

The Year 2003

Foreword

The Desert Journal's investigative reporting team of Bill Johnson, Fred Mramor and David Pierre are honored to present their months or years of work on the David Parker Ray Trail of Sexual Torture case in a series of articles spanning more than four years from late March 1999 to August 2003.

The initial works by this team—dated from late March to the end of June 1999—won first place in the Investigative Reporting category of the New Mexico Press Association's 1999 Better Newspaper Contest for Class 2 Weeklies. Judges were the Oklahoma Press Association, who commented on the DJ's entry, "Excellent coverage—excellent team effort. On sensation side—Does the public have the right to know [about] Satanism?" The judges scored the series at 97%.

We are providing this book of our investigative series because of the numerous inquiries we've received since the two books, *Cries in the Desert* by John Glatt and *Slow Death* by Jim Fielder, recently broke on bookshelves across America. People want to know what really happened and how this infamous crime case unfolded in one of New Mexico's premier prize-winning newspapers, the Desert Journal.

Most of our stories on the David Ray case did not make it on our online news service at www.desertjournalonline.com because of timing. The David Parker Ray case broke in March 1999 but Desert Journal Online wasn't established until more than two years later in May 2001. That's why this book project is so important—it brings it altogether in one package.

The following is an excerpt from the Desert Journal's cover letter, dated July 21, 1999, to the contest judges of the Oklahoma Press Association, who judged the NMPA's 1999 contest:

The horrifying story of a young woman who escaped an Elephant Butte residence wearing only a padlocked collar and chain around her neck after being kidnapped from Albuquerque and sexually tortured three days in March 1999 opened perhaps one of New Mexico's largest criminal investigations in years. The case has since exploded, revealing three more victims and a total of four suspects now awaiting justice—David Ray, his daughter Jessy Ray, his girlfriend Cindy Hendy and Roy Yancy, who is the only one charged so far with murder—his victim being a young mother of two small children, Marie Parker.

Since the inception of the case with the first arrests of David Ray and Cindy Hendy, the Desert Journal has been hot on the trail after leads—information which otherwise has escaped competing local, statewide and national press. The DJ team of Bill Johnson, Fred Mramor and David Pierre hereby submits their single entry for investigative reporting, spanning 11 weekly issues, some containing multiple stories, from late March to the end of June [1999].

The investigative efforts of the Desert Journal trio have revealed more possible suspects and victims—both alive and dead—and more leads to fuel the police investigation in solving this enormous case, which spans into several states. It also reveals the dark side of the human soul when it appears to dabble, or practice more fully, in the occult.

The four-part series, "Profile of a Satanist," which is included in this entry, takes a look at the satanic movement while also making a conclusion with the David Ray case. The Desert Journal's series concludes that occult-related activity or crime may be a driving force, or at least a contributing factor, behind the multiple kidnapping and sexual torture case (and, in Yancy's case, a murder and the investigation of another possible homicide victim to which he has been tied as a likely suspect).

With the police investigation still in its infancy, the Desert Journal expects to stay hot on the trail for a long time.

Respectfully Submitted,

Bill Johnson
Editor & Co-Publisher

...Confessions of a victim

"We decided to grab a beer at the local pub around the corner and while I went to the restroom you sneakily put some damned pill or powder in my drink because ten minutes after I drank just one beer, I started to get really tired and groggy and we agreed to leave the bar and return to your room for what I thought would be a friendly chat.

"A chat turned short and I was out cold. But sometime during the night, in the middle of captivity, your big fat blob of a body was on top of mine—then only half your size, or less! I could feel your crushing weight suffocating my puny body then as I lay under you on your bed—you, a trusted friend violated me.

"I said or yelled, "No! No! No!" and struggled with what little strength I had under the drug-induced state you put me under, but you continued to rape me and the next thing I'm out cold again and the early evening becomes late morning the next day and for some reason I wake up in your bed. I was a little freaked but I didn't remember the events of that night—not even of the five to ten seconds that I twenty years later would remember of those horrible things you did to me—never mind while I was unconscious and for how long and in what manner—and how I ached, was sore, felt physically mutilated by the incident but not knowing what happened for a whole 20 years..."

—A quote from one of the victims in this book

"It didn't happen that way!" said former state parks maintenance employee David Parker Ray, 59, of Elephant Butte (shown escorted by Sheriff's Office Captain Earl Easterling and Sheriff Terry Byers), in denying wrongdoing in the kidnapping, rape and torture of a young Albuquerque woman earlier this week.

Escape of kidnapping & rape victim ends three-day escapade at EB Lake

State parks employee and Elephant Butte woman arrested on multiple felony charges: bond for both set at $1 million cash only

By Bill Johnson of the Desert Journal
Friday, March 26, 1999

A state parks employee and an Elephant Butte woman allegedly kidnapped a 22-year-old Albuquerque woman and took her to Elephant Butte where she was raped and tortured three days before she escaped her tormentors, according to criminal complaints filed Tuesday in magistrate court.

State police leveled multiple felony charges against David Parker Ray, a 59-year-old maintenance employee at Elephant Butte Lake State Park, and his alleged accomplice in the crimes, Cynthea Lea Hendy, 39, also of Elephant Butte. Magistrate Thomas Pestak of Truth or Consequences Wednesday set cash only bonds at $1 million for each defendant.

Both defendants told news reporters before their first appearance Wednesday afternoon in the magistrate court of Truth or Consequences that they're innocent. "It didn't happen that way," said Ray when reporters questioned him about his innocence.

"I'm innocent... I'm afraid to talk," alleged accomplice Cindy Hendy, 39, also of Elephant Butte (shown in photo with a TV news reporter) told reporters as she was being escorted by detention officers to the magistrate court in Truth or Consequences.

DJ photos by David Pierre and Bill Johnson

"I'm innocent," Hendy said, adding moments later, "I'm afraid to talk..."

During their arraignments, held separately, Judge Pestak advised Ray and Hendy that they're exposed to serving a total of 93 years in state prison and paying a total of $85,000 in fines if convicted of all seven felony counts.

The victim, whose identity is being kept anonymous, escaped Monday afternoon from Ray's residence at 513 Bass Road overlooking Elephant Butte Lake where she had been held captive in chains and a metal collar and tortured with bare back whippings and electric shocks to her body for three days, according to the complaint.

The victim was alone with Cindy Hendy while Ray was at work and took advantage of being restrained then by only the metal collar. When she fled she was nude and wearing only the collar and while escaping a scuffle ensued whereby Hendy struck the victim on the head with a lamp. The victim said she struck Hendy's head with an ice pick, according to the arrest warrant affidavit filed by State Police Agent Wesley LaCuesta.

A dispatcher with the Sierra County Regional Dispatch Authority Monday afternoon deployed Sheriff Deputy David Elston to a 911 hang-up call at 513 Bass Road, informing the deputy that he heard commotion in the background. While Elston was on his way there, the dispatcher then told the deputy of a report of a naked woman running on the road and then being at a residence at 301 Springland.

After Deputies Elston and Lucas Alvarez arrived at the Bass Road residence they found the rear sliding glass door unlocked and with assistance of a state park ranger they cleared the home for any endangered persons.

"While clearing the residence, Deputy Elston said he observed, in plain view, various sexual devices and restraints in a bedroom. He said the assisting state park ranger identified the residence as belonging to Ray, who is also employed by the New Mexico State Parks," LaCuesta said in the affidavit.

Ray told Judge Pestak that his employment with state parks ended Tuesday.

Both suspects were located together in a camper vehicle driven by Ray, a park ranger informed Agent LaCuesta. A cut and dried blood also were observed on the back of Hendy's head and the back of her shirt, the affidavit said.

Deputy Alvarez found the victim, then wearing a pink robe, coming out of the Springland Road residence while in a "hysterical state, and screaming she had been kidnapped and locked up for three days."

Alvarez reported she had minor cuts and bruises on her body and a bump on her head. She also had a metal type collar around her neck that was secured with a padlock. A metal chain was attached to the collar, which was cut off at Sierra Vista Hospital's emergency room in T or C.

LaCuesta interviewed the victim and also observed small cuts on both of her legs, bruises on her right arm and bruising and an abrasion on both of her wrists. He also noticed welt type marks on her back and small puncture wounds and light bruising on her chest.

The victim told the agent she was on Central Avenue in Albuquerque between 10 a.m. and 11 a.m. last Saturday (March 20) when an acquaintance introduced her to Ray and Hendy, meeting in a recreational vehicle.

"David Ray showed her a small badge and told her she was under arrest for solicitation," according to the affidavit, adding that Hendy then came out of the restroom and handcuffed the victim, who then was restrained to a fixture inside the camper.

Hendy told Albuquerque's Channel 13 news reporter Wednesday, "Yeah, she (the victim) was a prostitute."

"The suspects then stripped her of her clothing and threatened to shock her with an electrical type device," the agent's affidavit said.

The victim said she was then taken to an unknown residential location where she was restrained by her legs and arms to a bed. The affidavit explicitly describes how Ray then raped the victim with the sexual devices while Hendy watched and "waved a small revolver at her threatening she would shoot her if she tried to escape."

The victim also told the agent that when she was escorted to the bathroom, Ray carried the same revolver with him.

"She described receiving 'shock therapy' in which two occasions, Ray would attach electrical type connections to her breasts, which would send electrical shocks through her body. Again, Cindy Hendy would look on as this occurred and assisted in keeping her restrained," the affidavit said.

Then last Sunday, according to the affidavit, both Hendy and Ray "whipped her on her back with a leather object with straps as she was restrained and hung from the ceiling." After the whipping, Ray again raped the victim with the sexual devices, the affidavit alleged.

The victim said she heard Hendy refer to Ray as David and Ray refer to Hendy as Cindy.

Felony charges filed against Ray include a count of first degree kidnapping, three counts of first degree criminal sexual penetration, a count of third degree assault with intent to commit a violent felony, and two counts of second degree conspiracy (to the crimes of kidnapping and criminal sexual penetration).

Felony charges filed against Hendy include a count of first degree kidnapping, three counts of first degree accessory to the crime of criminal sexual penetration, a count of third degree assault with intent to commit a violent felony and two counts of second degree conspiracy (to the crimes of kidnapping and criminal sexual penetration).

Hendy told Judge Pestak Wednesday she wants an attorney and that she can't afford to hire one because she lives on Social Security Income of $331 monthly.

Ray said he too couldn't afford his own attorney—now having lost his $550 take home check every other week; although he owns his mobile home, a 1985 Dodge, 1978 Toyota, a motor home, sail boat and power boat, altogether worth about $10,000 (according to the indigent form Ray filled out).

Ray said he didn't own the property on Bass Road because it's a lease lot at Elephant Butte Lake State Park. Ray also told the judge he's divorced and single but lives with his fiancé (Hendy).

Pestak told Ray he would notify him in a day or two to tell him whether he qualifies as an indigent to receive the free legal counsel of a public defender.

The magistrate court in T or C set preliminary hearings for both Ray and Hendy on a trail docket at 10 a.m. Wednesday, March 31. The court then will decide whether there is probable cause to bind over the defendants to district court for trial.

Not ruling out local perpetrators connected to David Ray and Cindy Hendy, Doug Beldon, supervisory special agent for the FBI, said, "Local names have not been mentioned by the FBI or New Mexico State Police." He addressed the large press corps gathered outside Ray's residence in Elephant Butte Tuesday afternoon.

Photo by David Pierre

Crime scene tape surrounds the Ray residence in Elephant Butte where 100 criminal investigators search for clues and evidence.

Photo by David Pierre

Second victim surfaces in kidnap-rape case

By Bill Johnson of the Desert Journal
Friday, April 2, 1999

A Truth or Consequences mother picking up a cake mix from her friends in Elephant Butte became the first known victim of Dennis Parker Ray and Cindy Lea Hendy a month before they kidnapped and raped their second victim who blew the lid wide open on a most bizarre and horrifying case after her narrow escape to safety March 22.

Angie, as she has been identified in earlier reports, was sexually tortured five days in February as her tormentors zapped her with "shock therapy" as they did their second victim—both identified as the first two of a possible myriad of victimized sex slaves—according to a criminal complaint filed Tuesday in the state district court in Truth or Consequences

Ray, 59, a mechanic at Elephant Butte Lake State Park until his arrest nearly two weeks ago, and his live-in girlfriend, Cindy Hendy, 39, of 513 Bass Road at Elephant Butte Lake State Park, are accused of the kidnapping and rapes of the two young Hispanic women, the second being age 22 and living in Albuquerque where she was abducted by Ray and Hendy on the morning of March 20.

Blue tarp surrounds the Elephant Butte residence of David Ray where FBI agents and state police attempt to work in obscurity while attracting the national press corps.

Photo by David Pierre

Meanwhile, a region wide investigation has expanded to Tucson and Phoenix, AZ, and Victoria and El Paso, TX, where Federal Bureau of Investigations agents are looking for clues or more victims after collecting more than 1,000 pieces of evidence from Ray's residence and lease lot since last week.

One of those pieces of evidence, according to John Ashbaugh, investigator for the District Attorney's Office, includes a photograph of Angie that police found in Ray's residence.

"[Angie] was pictured restrained with her body being stretched with torture instruments," according to Ashbaugh's affidavit for probable cause.

Ashbaugh said state police and FBI agents interviewed Angie last Sunday—six days after the arrests of Ray and Hendy on March 22 in connection with crimes they allegedly committed against their second victim.

Angie revealed that she went to Ray's and Hendy's residence Feb. 17 to pick up the cake mix. "Once she was inside with Hendy, Ray left for a few minutes and returned with a knife, pulled the knife on [Angie] and advised her that she was being kidnapped and held against her will," according to the investigator's affidavit.

The local and national news media get a photo op at David Ray's lease lot residence in Elephant Butte Tuesday afternoon.
DJ photo by David Pierre

Angie looked at Hendy and noticed Hendy was holding a gun on her. She was then stripped of her clothes and bound with a metal neck collar and other restraints as was their second victim a month later, according to the affidavit.

Angie was kept in a room in the residence where she had occasional contact with Ray and Hendy until the third day of captivity when they took her to a trailer outside the residence and secured her to a table with restraints.

"Inside the trailer on the walls were numerous restraint devices and medical tools," Ashbaugh's affidavit said.

After being secured to the table, Ray raped her with a sexual device while Hendy watched. After the carnage, they returned to the house and again secured their victim, Ashbaugh said.

The next day, Feb. 21, Angie "was forced to commit fellatio on Ray while Hendy watched," according to the affidavit.

She was later taken again to the trailer and again secured to the stretching table when Ray, with Hendy assisting, "hooked up electrodes or electric clips to [the private areas] and proceeded to run currents of electricity through her body. She was then taken back into the residence by both Ray and Hendy," the affidavit said.

What's in back of David Ray's mobile home? This evidence processor should know.

Photo by David Pierre

A couple of days later Angie was able to convince her captors to let her free. She was taken somewhere along Interstate 25 and released, the affidavit said, adding, "Officers have verified that she was picked up by a law enforcement officer and reported the events of the past few days to the officer."

Angie, camouflaged by a screen, told KOAT-TV news reporters Wednesday that she never got a return call or visit from the detective whom she thought would follow up on her report.

The "amended" criminal complaints filed Tuesday in district court leveled 25 felony counts each against both Ray and Hendy including 11 new felony counts related to Angie's case and seven new felony counts—in addition to the seven previously filed in magistrate court March 23—for a total of 14 felonies related to the case involving the second victim.

Charges filed against Ray and Hendy are identical and include two counts each of kidnapping and conspiracy to commit kidnapping, five counts each of criminal sexual penetration in the first or second degrees and aggravated battery, three counts each of conspiracy to commit criminal sexual penetration in the first or second degrees and conspiracy to commit aggravated battery, three counts of criminal sexual contact and two counts of conspiracy to commit criminal sexual contact.

Deputy District Attorney James A. Yontz of Socorro, who approved the criminal complaints, also filed a motion for the defendants to join in a common cause number. His basis for the request, according to the motion, is that each defendant is charged with accountability for each offense included in the complaints and that all of the defendants are charged with conspiracy as part of a common scheme or plan. Yontz added that Rule 5-203 B mandates that these cases shall be joined.

Magistrate Judge Thomas Pestak set bond for the co-defendants at $1 million cash only during their first appearance in court March 24. Both Ray and Hendy then told the press they're innocent.

FBI agents scour the rear of David Ray's mobile home in Elephant Butte Tuesday morning for clues.

DJ photos by David Pierre

Close friend to David Ray considers herself lucky

Says her affection for 'Dad' may have prevented harm

By Bill Johnson of the Desert Journal
Friday, April 2, 1999

Becky says she considers herself very lucky having avoided the snares of her friend's father whom she had called "Dad" in spite of David Parker Ray's protests.

Now Becky, a young woman of Truth or Consequences, says she has nightmares every night or since the arrests of Ray, 59, and his girlfriend, Cindy Hendy, 39, in connection with the kidnapping and rape of a 22-year-old Albuquerque woman March 20 to 22 at their Elephant Butte residence.

An ongoing investigation involving 100 state police officers and Federal Bureau of Investigations agents, which has attracted state and national news media, has disclosed a second kidnapping and rape torture victim from Truth or Consequences and additional charges were filed Tuesday against Ray and Hendy.

Becky, who wished to keep her identity anonymous and whose authenticity can be verified by the Desert Journal, said during a phone interview Tuesday morning that she now thinks that Ray's mannerisms, behavior and speech were rather peculiar and that she could have been very likely targeted as another of his sex slave victims.

Identifying herself as a close friend to the family, Becky said she had lived at the home of her friend, Glenda Ray, and her father, David Ray, at 513 Bass Road at Elephant Butte Lake State Park about a week but noticed nothing out of the ordinary then. Describing herself as being generally unobservant of her surroundings during her week's stay, she said, "Nothing was weird then, but nothing made me uncomfortable."

Becky said that when Glenda and her father went out on the lake in their sailboat, they would say it was ladies day out—"only women allowed and no men except David Ray. He was the only man allowed."

"I sailed with David Ray a couple of times and one time he tied a rope around my ankle in a knot. He took the slack in the rope from around the sails and wrapped it around my ankle and said, 'I got you now!' I took the rope tying around my ankle as a joke. It wasn't tight, I could pull my feet out."

Becky said she spoke with Sheriff Deputy Glenn Hamilton after Ray's and Hendy's arrests. "The police wanted to know my connection. They haven't gotten back with me yet," she said Tuesday.

It was during these sailing excursions that Ray would reveal his morbid inner thoughts, according to Becky.

"I remember when I went out on the lake with him he (Ray) said several times, "This is the deepest parts," Becky said. She added, however, that she can't remember exactly where the deepest parts are located although Black Bluffs and Mitchell Point were places they went to while sailing on Elephant Butte Lake.

Becky said that one time she was telling Ray about how an ex-boyfriend was stalking her and how she wished she could stop him.

"Ray told me the best way to get rid of a stalker is to open them, put rocks in them, wrap chicken wire around them and drop them to the bottom of the lake," Becky said.

On another sailing trip, Becky said she asked one time, "If the dam broke do you think they would find bodies (on the bottom of the lake)? Ray said, 'You bet. There's lots of bodies at the bottom of the lake."

"Every night recently I wake up. I used to call Ray 'Dad.' I knew he was a pervert, but he left me alone," she said.

Becky said she was walking alone one time on Rock Canyon Road near the lake when Ray saw her and pulled over in his vehicle, got out and "begged me not to walk out alone at the lake. And he said, '200 girls a year have something happen to them out here.' He picked me up and put me in his vehicle—a white Dodge Ranger—and gave me a ride."

Becky said police told her that "15 to 20 girls a year—not 200—may have something happen to them out there. It could have been his guilty conscience that led to his tears when he begged me not to walk out alone."

Becky said that Glenda and David Ray would bring home "hundreds I've seen who were hitch hikers." She said a man known as "Peter Pan" and a girl from Albuquerque, who went by the name of "New York," were at Ray's residence one time. "They said they dropped her (New York) off in Albuquerque. She aggravated Dad (Ray) when she was there."

Lastly, during one of her last visits to the Ray's residence in February, Becky said she went with a friend, who works at the New Mexico Veterans Center in Truth or Consequences, to pay Ray back on a personal loan. "He rushed us off."

"I think Angie (one of Ray's and Hendy's alleged kidnapping and rape victims) was there then when he victimized her," Becky said, adding that from news accounts she understood that Ray and Hendy kept Angie at their home five days in February—the reason perhaps that Becky and her friend didn't get a warm welcome and instead were rushed off.

"I told Hamilton I had a hard time believing he (Ray or Dad) did this," Becky said. She added that Hamilton responded, "Not only is Ray guilty but Glenda is too" and that police had videotapes to prove it.

Becky said she understood that Glenda Ray, whose street name is Jesse, and a Sandy Rivera went to Big Springs, TX, together. "Ray's ex-wife also lives in Big Springs."

However, unconfirmed information from other sources put Glenda Ray in Arizona or in the near vicinity "hiding out."

Nonetheless, Becky said, "I think my love for him (Ray) prevented my harm. He constantly told me, 'Don't call me Dad'!"

Becky said her story is true and added, "I buried an engine with Jesse in the front yard." She said that police during their weeklong excavation of Ray's yard should have uncovered the engine by now.

Becky said she is known to the Desert Journal because she had helped Glenda Ray write an article about an injured bird Glenda had rescued at the lake a couple of years ago and that she also went with Glenda to deliver the article to the newspaper office in T or C.

<<< >>>

The Truth or Consequences City Council Chambers fills up with citizens concerned about the media blitz on the David Ray sexual torture case at Elephant Butte Lake.

DJ photo by Bill Johnson

Community safe again, authorities tell town folk

But evasive about their probe for clues of a possible serial killer

By Bill Johnson of the Desert Journal
Friday, April 2, 1999

Despite long winded, evasive "no comments" about the progress of the pending investigation by state police and Federal Bureau of Investigations agents into what many in the local and national press corps now believe may become a top billing on their charts with the story of a possible serial killer evolving, state authorities say they believe Elephant Butte and Truth or Consequences are safe again with the arrests of two suspects.

About a hundred law enforcement officers from various agencies, including the FBI's criminal profiling team from Quantico, VA, have converged on Elephant Butte and neighboring Truth or Consequences in an effort to piece together more than a thousand items of evidence found at the residence of David Parker Ray, 59, and his girlfriend, Cindy Hendy, 39, at 513 Bass Road in Elephant Butte, following their arrests March 22 in connection with the kidnappings and rapes of two women in February and March, according to Dave Kitchen, special agent in charge of the FBI's Albuquerque office.

"We'll be at the crime scene at least three more days. We won't leave no stone unturned," said Kitchen Tuesday night before a standing-room-only audience with eight different TV news crews including the big national networks and syndications in the T or C Civic Center's Council Chambers. "New Mexico State Police and the FBI have resources deployed."

New Mexico Department of Public Safety Darren White, who led the public meeting to address citizens' concerns, however, seemed more inclined to pitch the community as being a safer one now that Ray and Hendy are behind bars.

"I wish it was under a different set of circumstances that we hold this town hall meeting," White said.

"We're here to address your fears and rumors that have become frenzied since last Wednesday (March 24). We come here tonight to say T or C and Elephant Butte is a safe community with wonderful people who live here. I come to recreate here every summer," White said.

Although none of the authorities would confirm rumors of massive "homicidal" rape, White said, "This current situation could be the community's worst nightmare. We won't allow this to demonize New Mexico."

White said the community has a right to know what's going on while "we preserve the integrity of this investigation. We want to share several things you might encounter in the next several days, weeks or months—this investigation may take that long."

Frank Taylor, Chief of New Mexico State Police in Santa Fe, said Kitchen's FBI agents have been considerably helpful in the probe. He said District Attorney Ron Lopez also has made himself available 24 hours daily at the command post to ensure that proper steps are taken.

Taylor said that of the 100 lawmen deployed here, 20 are state police officers. "It's a very complex investigation. We want to make sure we don't leave any stone unturned. I can understand how you (the community) feel—scared."

"We don't know if this extends beyond a rape-kidnapping case," Taylor said, but adding that if anyone has any information involving the suspects they should come forward and talk. "We aren't an occupying force. We're here to help you… anytime in situations like this."

White said people with information, whether rumor or hearsay, should call either Lt. Newman or Lt. Bertrand locally at 744-4295.

Taylor said that information and rumors will be forthcoming such as about bodies coming to the surface. "But be patient with us," he added.

"The case requires considerable resources… It's a complex crime scene. El Paso sent its evidence response team and we collected over 1,000 pieces of evidence," Kitchen said.

The scope of the investigation also may spread to other areas. According to White, "We're not ruling out there may be other victims from the region or other states." He said there are also a lot of rumors of burial sites and bodies in Elephant Butte Lake. "Those are rumors. Our investigations are checking up on 100 leads in this case. This case is complex—it involves some things people shouldn't have to witness. We uncovered things that are very disturbing."

White said New Mexico is the sixth most violent state in the nation. "It's high profile cases like this one that draws people (news media). We all have to get involved about how violent our state is."

Elephant Butte Mayor Bob Barnes asked how an investigation into a kidnapping-rape case evolves into rumors of mass murder and serial killers. "How does this happen?"

"When we got preliminary information we realized this was beyond our scope and realized it would be a very difficult case. If this case involves dark and disturbing facts… The news media knows that when there are 60 to 100 investigators on a case, there's something big going on," White responded. "If you hear rumors, call and we can tell whether they're true or not."

When asked by a citizen about any possible body recoveries, White said, "It's not true we removed 14 bodies from the lake. To the credit of the news media, they don't want to report inaccurately. They'll try to verify information. There will be an anonymous source from time to time—that will happen."

Desert Journal reporter Fred Mramor asked, "Was Ray involved with Marie Parker (a young T or C mother) or her disappearance (from the lake area in July 1997)?"

"We cannot disclose that," White said, again stating that police must preserve the integrity of a pending investigation by remaining mute. "Agents will go through numerous reports, including missing persons reports. If you have information you think we need to know, call us."

White said it has been impossible for police to respond to all of the calls coming in. "It pains me to hear the rumors about the lake. We don't need to demonize the lake."

Asked by a citizen about Ray's record, White said, "We won't discuss Ray's criminal record (although it is a matter of public record with public access)." White said also, "I won't say that other communities are involved but they are a part of compiling the suspect's history. We won't discuss our victims, for example, their alleged life styles (statements such as the Albuquerque kidnap-rape victim was a prostitute, according to Hendy). They're protected in the State of New Mexico. We know there are more victims out there."

When asked about whether videotapes taken by the suspects of their alleged crimes reveal more victims or suspects, White said, "We won't discuss the specific details of evidence, such as whether videotapes show other crimes, etc."

"The community is safer. We enjoy a peaceful life and want to go back to that," White said.

DA Lopez reminded the crowd that police and prosecutors can't make improper statements on the investigation and evidence.

"Most of the officers on this case are criminal agents. The motels know who they are. We could barely get a room here," White said.

Elephant Butte City Council member Mike McAfee asked what evidence triggered the complexity in the case.

"It was in the criminal complaint," White said. "We're not usually at the crime scene a whole week."

One citizen then tried to nail down where the community is on a disaster scale of 1 to 100.

"We're on the lower end," White said. "What's comforting in this case is that we have two suspects behind bars. That does not minimize the damage and destruction caused by these suspects. There could be unthinkable things that happened to people."

"This is the number one priority for the Department of Public Safety and the FBI," White said. "I don't want to say these weren't horrific crimes. I won't downplay that people were horribly victimized."

In answering Las Palomas resident Don Velzy's question about usurping Sheriff Terry Byers of his authority or responsibilities, White said, "They (Sheriff's Office) recognized the complexity of the case and called us in. It's no reflection on any agency in this county. More agencies may be called in. Kitchen brought profilers in because this case expands beyond this community."

Byers said the Sheriff's Office lacks the resources to handle cases such as this one. "It didn't take long to say we can't handle this. We are investigating but not to the extent that the state police and FBI are," Byers said.

On a somber note, the town hall meeting was adjourned with promises of daily meetings with the press: more rumors, more "no comments" and more waiting.

<<< >>>

Satellite communications pop up on Truth or Consequences' landscape—this time downtown—with the media coverage of the David Ray case.

DJ photo by David Pierre

Law agencies, media descend upon area

By David Pierre of the Desert Journal
Friday, April 2, 1999

Law enforcement agencies and the news media have converged on Truth or Consequences and Elephant Butte area for the second time in a month.

Still mourning the shooting death of Sheriff Deputy Kelly Clark March 4, now Sierra County residents face the unfolding of horrific crimes that attract more attention than they want.

If the amount of national and even international coverage the area has experienced is any indication, the siege may continue for weeks, perhaps months, to some extent.

Dozens of New Mexico State Police personnel began their investigation of the alleged kidnapping and torture case of a 22-year-old Albuquerque woman that landed David Parker Ray and Cindy Hendy in the Sierra County Jail on a $1 million cash only bond each after their victim escaped.

That opened the door for the Federal Bureau of Investigations and more state police to infiltrate the crime scene.

By Tuesday, the FBI had sent behavioral specialists to the area to assess the situation of a possible multiple murder case.

The specialists referred to as "profilers" were made famous by movies and television.

Additionally, reports of bone fragments and human remains at the residence of Ray and Hendy in Elephant Butte grabbed the interest of the national media.

Reporter Mark Horner of KRQE Channel 13 in Albuquerque who first broke the story for TV told the Desert Journal last Monday, "I think you're about to have network crews, with their satellite trucks, descend on your town."

After a national spot on CBS Tuesday morning, Horner became one of dozens of reporters pouring into the community hoping for a lead to a story which law enforcement agencies have produced no concrete proof of homicide.

To further cloud the investigation, bone fragments found in Ray's yard, marked by foot high orange flags, turned out to not be that of human remains. But the excavation continues.

On Tuesday's photo opportunity at the crime scene where more than a couple of dozen reporters and photographers were present, state police Lt. R.L. Bertram said while there was yet a large volume of evidence, "The bones were not human."

Still, with the possibility of this being a nationwide mass murder case, media from all over the country remained and kept coming to Sierra County. "With possible victims in different areas of the country this is important to a lot of media," said one state police officer.

Asked how long the investigators will be at the crime scene, Bertram said, "Quite a while longer, it depends on exactly what they find."

Bertram also asked for help from the Tucson and Phoenix media. "We're investigating and we need help. If anyone knows anything about this case we are asking them to come forth," added Bertram.

So it seemed as if law enforcement was allowing the media to help find other victims without really throwing them a bone.

"Imagine the worst thing that could happen to you… that wouldn't even compare," said Deputy District Attorney Jim Yontz of Socorro when asked if the media was here in vain.

In terms of media from outside areas, KOLD-TV of Tucson, KTUK-TV of Phoenix, The Dallas Morning News, CBS, ABC, NBC network affiliates, The New York Times, Associated Press, and Reuters America in addition to the Spanish TV Station, Hard Copy and Extra TV news shows have arrived with visions of torture and homicide dancing in their heads.

Rumors in the area have ranged from David Ray opening victims' bodies, filling them with rocks, wrapping them with chicken wire and dropping them to the bottom of Elephant Butte Lake on his weekly boat trips to the middle of the lake to a possible refrigerator in Ray's trailer filled with meat possibly that of human remains. Other rumors have indicated that maybe previous residents of Sierra County could have been in on the crimes.

However, law officials did find a videotaped orientation, apparently shown to victims so they would know what to expect. According to the Albuquerque Journal, the tape was said to have, "I bet you're scared and we're going to play with you for awhile."

Doug Beldon, supervisory special agent for the FBI, said, not ruling out local perpetrators connected to Ray and Hendy, "Local names have not been mentioned by the FBI or New Mexico State Police."

A local motel manager who said he knew Ray told the Desert Journal, "I knew him. I've been hounded by all of them (media). The thing that pisses me off is that it's all because of this," he said pointing to his nose. Asked about Hendy, he said, "She's a crank freak."

Though the conversation was sketchy, when asked if in his opinion Ray has done all of the things rumored by the public, including disposing of bodies, he indicated yes.

But public opinion and media speculation are one thing. Hard facts from investigators to date remain sparse.

However at least one other victim referred to as "Angie" has come forth producing interviews with several media.

Mike Simon, a cameraman for Good Morning America, said, "Yeah, we interviewed her (Angie) live in room 112 of the Super 8 motel. We took a sheet off the bed and hung it up. We used some blue back lighting to create a silhouette (to preserve anonymity) and we shot it."

Media interaction was rampant as many of the reporters just arriving hadn't a clue as to what the facts were.

Two reporters checking into a local motel, Stephanie Guadian and Mark Oltz of KTUK-TV in Phoenix observed other reporters. Looking at each other they said, "Network!" Referring to the type of "look" the reporters had, "You can tell... They're all serious... And what are they doing heading out to work at midnight?"

The next day Guadian said, "There's a lot of rumors out there but nothing we can report! But we'll stick around another day."

The next day would be April 1 and if the visiting media didn't get the information they were looking for then, the joke would be on them.

When asked if the media habitually jumped the gun when here weren't facts to back up such an interest, State Police information officer Richard Newman said, "I think they do but we're not used to it here in New Mexico," but added, "It's a very interesting case and people want to know about it."

Is the community really safe?

By Bill Johnson of the Desert Journal
Friday, April 9, 1999

Is it safe? The community, that is?

Well Darren White, Cabinet Secretary of the New Mexico Department of Public Safety, said recently it's safe with the arrests and incarceration of the two suspects accused of the kidnap, rape and torture of two women in the suspects' home at Elephant Butte Lake.

Now we can all let our hair down, call off the guard and dance naked in the streets because White says he won't let New Mexico, Elephant Butte Lake, or this community to become "demonized" at the hands of criminals. Could that be the reason for all of those cover-ups? Keep it out of the press and who'll care, no one will know?

The state's largest reservoir and recreation paradise has been known to have been used from time to time as a dumping grounds for killers disposing of their victims' bodies. Take for examples the unsolved mysteries surrounding the two homicide victims whose bodies came to surface nearly a decade ago: Janice Pulliam of Albuquerque and a John Doe, whose identity, we assume, is still unknown. Both victims' bodies were anchored down with weights of some kind and in John Doe's case, he was wrapped in tarpaulin and dropped into the lake with a boat anchor after being executed—shot in the back of the head.

Of course, these are very isolated incidents and shouldn't be used by anyone, including the press, to "demonize" the lake, although the ghosts of these victims will never rest without vengeance or justice bestowed upon their transgressors.

Yet, while Secretary White pitches the safeness of such recreational facilities (he sounds like the tourism czar), he also admits that New Mexico is the sixth most violent state in the nation. Well… the Hot Spot Crew congratulates the Public Safety Cabinet Secretary for making New Mexico "safer" after previous statistics showed New Mexico to be the seventh most violent state in the union.

Murder suspect Yancy dabbled in the occult

By Bill Johnson of the Desert Journal
Friday, April 16, 1999

The suspect arrested a week ago for allegedly strangling a 22-year-old Truth or Consequences woman to death nearly two years ago had dabbled with Satanism when he was a youth.

Dennis Roy Yancy, 27, of Williamsburg, was believed to have reformed from occult-related crimes he committed 12 years ago with several other cult members until he allegedly killed Marie Parker, the mother of two small children, in July 1997.

The murder is believed to be connected to the kidnap, torture-rape cases leveled against David Parker Ray, 59, and his girlfriend Cindy Hendy, 39, at their residence, 513 Bass Road at Elephant Butte Lake State Park. Investigators and attorneys refused to elaborate on the connection after Yancy's arraignment in magistrate court Monday.

"These kids—Yancy and crew—were involved in animal sacrifices. Now 12 years later they're allegedly killing people," said a former independent occult crimes specialist who spoke only on conditions of anonymity.

Yancy, who was a hardcore member of the small group, helped to build a small arsenal of stolen firearms that had been taken in burglaries, according to the specialist.

A Truth or Consequences man said he remembers the occult activity in the fall of 1987 because his son and Yancy had grown up together. Speaking only on conditions of anonymity, the father said, "Yancy and other kids burglarized Doc Woodard's house and stole computer equipment and other stuff. these kids were involved in Satanism." Woodard, he added, was a teacher at Hot Springs High School.

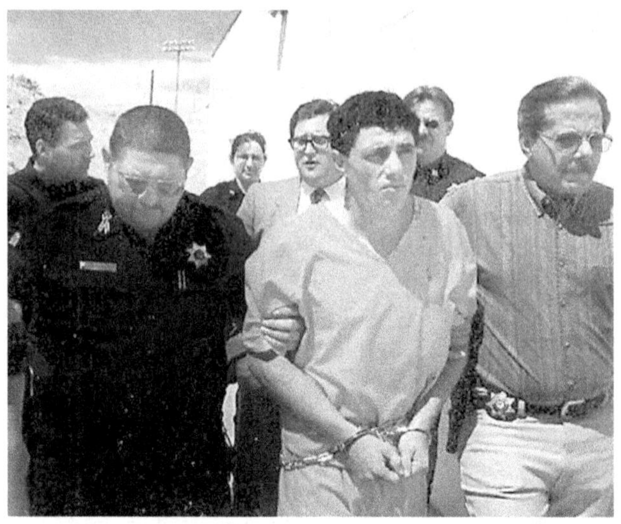

Accused of the murder of Marie Parker in July 1997, Roy Yancy—flanked by Sierra County Chief Detention Officer Jeff Fields and Jail Administrator Russell Peterson—leaves the magistrate court in Truth or Consequences Monday afternoon for the Dona Ana County Jail where he's being held without bond.

Photo by Bill Johnson

"They cut a dog's penis off and placed it on a computer and there was a satanic symbol," the man said.

A resident of Williamsburg said she remembers in the fall of 1987 how dogs—belonging to her community's residents with their last names starting with "R"—were poisoned to death.

The occult crimes specialist said he recalls that the stolen items, including guns, which Yancy and the other boys took, were found in a vacant lot and in one of the suspect's homes in either the attic or basement along with satanic literature and symbols, including a pentagram (five pointed star or goat's head).

"The parents said, 'These guns don't belong to us'," ending what could have become mayhem in Truth or Consequences, the specialist said.

However, it was not the end, as the teen satanic cult members went on a letter-writing campaign to seek out a possible virgin to sacrifice on Halloween, according to the unnamed authority on the occult. "Girls received the life-threatening notes with satanic symbols," he said.

"There was a big scare in the high school. The boys tried to get the girls to go with them by talking about the scare and saying how they would protect them from Satanists (such as themselves)," the occult crimes specialist said, adding, "None of the girls were stupid enough to go with them."

Because of the scare and the possibility of the boys being armed to the teeth and being a danger to society, a joint task force was created by the local district attorney's office, city police department, sheriff's office, state police and border patrol (the latter two being inactive members) to investigate allegations of satanic or occult related crimes in the area, according to the specialist who was a member of the task force.

In fact, it was this case involving Yancy that ultimately led the specialist to research the occult, publish a book exclusively for law enforcement agencies and become an occult crimes instructor with the American Police Academy—the training arm of the National Association of Chiefs of Police—in Washington, DC.

"We've always known these kids were involved in Satanism while in high school, but we never know what happens with these kids when they grow up because no one has ever been able to track this activity with their juvenile records being sealed," the specialist said.

Roy Yancy's wife, Christina, told news reporters that her husband was forced to strangle Marie Parker to death, emulating the alibi of "the devil made me do it." Shown with Mrs. Yancy is the family's friend, George Padilla.

Photo by David Pierre

"One thing I do remember about teenage Satanism is that the level of violence intensifies more rapidly than with other types of juvenile crime. Now it's 12 years later and they're involved in something real sick. It's no surprise that a little monster grows up to be a big monster," he said.

The specialist said his interview is exclusive to the Desert Journal but that he would be willing to talk to agents of the Federal Bureau of Investigations about Yancy's case, "although the FBI hasn't acknowledged the existence of occult-related crime the last five years."

Nadyne Gardner, who was Yancy's English teacher at the time, said she thought Yancy was bright but went the wrong direction with his life. She said she had made Yancy write a long essay on the history of Satanism to try to thwart his interest in the subject. She added that Yancy was a hyperactive kid "on Ritalin."

About two years after the satanic activity appeared to have ceased and while still in high school during the summer of 1989, Yancy coached tee-ball for youngsters, including this reporter's two stepchildren. It had seemed that Yancy had reformed himself because he worked really well with the small children. They really seemed to like him and the way he treated them as a coach. This reporter was particularly proud of the way Yancy was progressing into a young, healthy adult with a bright future ahead.

But clouds of evil would cast shadows of doubt on his straight and narrow pathway and Yancy again would get caught in the wrong crowd. And he would employ deception, as any Satan worshipper might to justify his means, as a front for his deviant, allegedly criminal behavior.

Shortly after Marie Parker's disappearance, according to the father of the son who was Yancy's friend, "My son (The father of one of Marie Parker's children) said Yancy told him that he (Yancy) saw Marie camped out at the lake and that she had told Yancy that she wanted to hitch a ride out of town. My son said he talked to T or C police (about Yancy's statement) but no report was written."

The father said he had heard at a local bar that Marie, the day before she came up missing, reported she had been raped. "A girl, Cynthia, took her to the police department to report the rape," he said, but adding, "That's hearsay."

The "devil-made-me-do-it" syndrome seems to be the alibi that Yancy's wife, Christina, is using to explain her husband's role in allegedly causing Parker's death.

Mrs. Yancy told news reporters that after her husband's arrest a week ago he confessed to her to having strangled Marie Parker but under orders of David Ray's daughter, Glenda "Jessy" Ray.

Mrs. Yancy said Glenda Ray held Marie down at gunpoint while

Glenda's father David Ray took photographs of her husband (Yancy) strangling her.

Yancy was ordered incarcerated without bond in the Dona Ana County Jail during his first appearance Monday before Sierra County Magistrate Thomas Pestak. Yancy's temporary attorney, Steve Sosa, entered a plea of not guilty to all of the charges filed against Yancy by state police agent Norman Rhoades.

Sosa said later Yancy will be represented by Ruidoso attorney Gary Mitchell, who specializes in such cases for the Public Defenders Office, since conviction on a capital murder charge carries a death penalty or life in prison.

Besides capital murder, other felony charges filed against Yancy include a count each of first degree kidnapping, second degree conspiracy to commit murder and conspiracy to commit kidnapping, and fourth degree tampering with evidence.

Pestak said if no death penalty is imposed, Yancy could face, upon conviction of all of the crimes, a life term plus 49 and one half years in prison, and $45,000 in fines.

Details surrounding the case are sketchy since District Attorney Ron Lopez said Monday the court sealed the statement of facts upon his request "so as not to prejudice Yancy's case."

Since conspiracy involves more than one person, charges apparently are pending against other suspects. But Lopez said, "I won't comment whether the statement of facts contains other suspects' names."

Lopez said another reason the affidavits have been sealed is because the judicial system otherwise would have to look at a change of venue to try Yancy's case. "Where will we try this case (with all of the worldwide attention through the news media)?" he asked. "It's in the best interest of the prosecution and pretrial publicity," he said.

Yancy told the judge he was employed only one day (as a cook at a local restaurant) when he was arrested last Friday night and that he has neither public assistance nor any income since he's no longer working.

Judge Pestak ruled Yancy qualifies for a public defender and waived his $10 application fee.

In arguing over bond arrangements, District Attorney Lopez said he wanted to continue no bond as set by the court when Yancy was arrested. He said the law allows the court at its discretion to hold a defendant without bond, especially in cases of a capital offense. "If Yancy is held without bond, there must be a preliminary hearing within 10 days," Lopez said.

In arguing for the court to set some kind of bond, Sosa said no evidence was presented to the court to justify no bond.

Pestak denied the defense attorney's request, granting no bond.

Meanwhile, a massive search party has been looking since Saturday for the body of Marie Parker whom investigators say was buried out in the desert near State Road 195 between Elephant Butte Lake and Interstate 25. Lopez said he believes he could still successfully prosecute the case without Parker's body being found.

Pablo Nuanes (above) had Marie Parker set up camp during a Fourth of July party at Elephant Butte Lake in 1997 before Roy Yancy allegedly strangled Parker to death.

DJ file photo by Lucille Benda

Informant blows whistle in Parker's murder case

By Bill Johnson of the Desert Journal
Friday, April 16, 1999

Marie Parker of Truth or Consequences thought she was going to Elephant Butte Lake to have a week full of fun in the sun during the Fourth of July holiday two years ago. Instead, the 22-year-old mother of two children disappeared from the face of the earth, apparently not of her own choice as many people had been led to believe.

With last Friday's arrest of Dennis Roy Yancy, 27, of Williamsburg, in connection with the kidnapping and capital murder of Parker, at least one predominant question is being asked by the news media and public over the conspiracy charges that also were filed against him. Who are the other suspects in this case?

Since the magistrate court sealed all of the criminal information or statement of facts in Yancy's case upon District Attorney Ron Lopez's request, the question will remain unanswered until formal charges are filed in a court of law—at which time these allegations are to be made public record.

A reliable confidential informant, however, came forward this week to reveal a wealth of information surrounding the circumstances of Marie Parker's disappearance and apparent murder. Apparent because her body still has not surfaced in a massive search that began last Saturday in the desert between the lake and Interstate 25l. The informant's statement was provided exclusively for the Desert Journal, state police and agents of the Federal Bureau of Investigations.

According to the informant, Pablo Nuanes of Truth or Consequences had invited Marie Parker to a Fourth of July party at the lake in 1997.

"Nuanes played a big part in getting her to be at that party by putting her in charge of setting up camp on Tuesday of that week (Friday being the 4th). When I asked Pablo where everyone—Jessy Ray, Marie Parker and another man, all of whom the informant kept company with for a week or two before the party—was after the party ended he (Nuanes) said they would be back in a couple of hours because they were cleaning up the camp site."

The informant said that after Parker was reported missing and people were calling in leads as to her whereabouts, Nuanes, a known crank dealer and user, moved to Farmington where the other man (whom the informant had kept company with before the party) also had moved to about two to four weeks earlier. Nuanes eventually returned to T or C.

The informant said that about a year and a half ago or a few months after Parker's disappearance, of which she constantly inquired, the informant was invited to somebody's home to play pool. "After I was there for about one hour Pablo took out a weapon and started about 'rats' and how with that weapon he could take any of them out, the whole time looking for my reaction. I went to a local business the next evening and two white males made the comment to me, 'Look who's still alive'."

The informant said that about six months after Parker was reported missing, Nuanes told her that he had heard on the news that the body of Parker was found (possibly in Socorro). "Another man was present for that conversation and he said he also heard that on the news, and now I could stop wondering what happened to Marie Parker," the informant said. The informant added that she thinks now that Nuanes told her that information as a front, possibly to cover up something.

The informant said Glenda "Jessy" Ray—the daughter of David Parker Ray, who is accused with his girlfriend Cindy Hendy on the kidnap-torture rape of two women in February and March at Ray's home at Elephant Butte Lake State Park—"keeps a lot of company with Pablo Nuanes" and that Jessy Ray also helped in the details of the Fourth of July party.

"Jessy Ray was one of the last persons (seen) with Marie Parker," the informant added.

The informant said Jessy Ray nine months ago invited her (informant) to meet her dad (David Ray) "after she apparently drugged me—slipped me a Mickey in a beer"—at an Elephant Butte establishment.

"We went to her house on Bass Road, I was introduced to her father and stayed about 10 minutes before we (informant and Jessy Ray) went to J&S Shamrock in David Ray's utility vehicle. We returned to her house and eventually she seemed to have lured me into her bedroom with David Ray following me. I didn't notice anything unusual but did see handcuffs on her bed post. I felt my guard was definitely up and decided to leave."

The informant said a man told her recently that the FBI interviewed him and that he told them Marie Parker had invited him to the Fourth of July party at the lake.

"When he got there he asked Pablo Nuanes where Marie Parker was and Nuanes told him that Marie Parker was asleep in the tent and Nuanes would not let him bother her. The man said he left after that."

The informant added that two men she knows spent a lot of time with Jessy Ray at their house and at Pablo Nuanes' house since they also are good friends of Nuanes. She said that the February victim of David Ray and Cindy Hendy, known as Angie, also frequently spent time at these two men's house.

"They have a cousin who told me that about two years ago he bought x-rated movies from someone in T or C. He said he sold them when he needed beer money. I saw the case the tape was in and it didn't look like it came from the manufacturer," the informant said.

The informant said these same two men are good friends with another man who also told her that he buys x-rated movies from someone in T or C "and discussed it with me thinking I knew what he was talking about."

The informant said her first encounter with Roy Yancy occurred in 1995. "He went to my residence, demanding to let him into my house. it was the first time I ever saw him. I refused to let him in, thinking he might case my home for items to be stolen at a later time."

The informant said Jessy Ray formally introduced her (informant) to Roy Yancy about a year ago.

Lastly, the informant said she was invited by Pablo Nuanes and Jessy Ray to the Fourth of July party at the lake but was unable to attend.

<<< >>>

District Attorney Ron Lopez said Monday he had the statement of facts sealed in the murder case involving Roy Yancy to prevent excessive pretrial publicity. He refused to say who the other suspects are in the conspiracy.

Photo by Bill Johnson

Ray's victim breaks down on stand

By Fred Mramor of the Desert Journal
Friday, April 16, 1999

Thursday's preliminary hearing for kidnap and sexual torture suspect David Parker Ray was interrupted by his victim's emotional outburst on the witness stand.

District Judge Neil Mertz cleared the Truth or Consequences courtroom for 20 minutes to allow the witness to regain her composure before returning to testify.

The victim, a 22-year-old Albuquerque woman, described her abduction by Ray, 59, and his alleged accomplice, Cindy Hendy, 39, both of Elephant Butte, from an Albuquerque parking lot on March 20.

She testified that she had gotten into his brown RV to sell sexual favors. Ray pulled out a badge and told her she was under arrest. She said Hendy held stun guns when Hendy came out of the RV's bathroom.

She said she was handcuffed and shackled and that she screamed and tried to escape, but Hendy pulled her hair, kicked her and pulled her back into the RV before they drove around for an hour.

They then stopped to switch drivers and also stripped her of her clothing and put a mask over her head, the victim testified.

The victim testified they drove for what seemed like hours and she ended up at a trailer. They took her into the trailer, still handcuffed and shackled, went into a den and they tied her to a bed, putting a metal collar and padlock around her neck.

Deputy District Attorney Jim Yontz put on a rubber glove to open a sealed evidence bag from which he produced a steel collar and chain.

He took the collar to the victim. She held it for a moment and threw the collar and chain down on the witness stand before her. She then began to cry uncontrollably.

The court officers scurried around and huddled while state victims' advocate Vicki Brodie attempted to comfort her. The victim then pointed towards David Ray and yelled, "You sorry bastard! How can you do this to me? You sorry bastard!" The spectators apparently were shaken by the victim's outburst.

After the 20-minute recess, the victim continued to testify that Ray and Hendy laid her on a bed with the collar and chain. They brought out a machine with wires and clips which they attached to her breasts and vagina. They shocked her with the device for about a half hour, she testified.

Next, Ray placed her on the floor and put gravy on her body, brought a dog in from outside. The dog licked the gravy off of her, she testified.

They put her back into the bed still restrained. She slept for what seemed like all night. "All I wanted to do was sleep," she said.

When she woke up she lay in bed for a long time before Ray put "leather things" around her waist and ankles. She said also she was suspended from a hook on the ceiling. Ray spread her legs apart with orange ropes and beat her with a belt and whips, she testified.

He got a steel object with "pokey things" which he stuck in her vagina and while doing so he also inserted another device, which expands and contracts, in her rectum, she testified. The victim said Hendy was present for the rape and torture sessions and held a handgun.

They took her into another room where she more or less was subjected to the same torture. She testified also that Ray had played an audiotape in which Ray described what was going to happen and why she was there.

She was left alone with Hendy on March 22. The victim said the collar still restrained her with the chain attached to a bar on the wall. She saw that the keys were left on a coffee table, which she tried to pull towards her with her legs.

Hendy saw her in the act, ran towards her and told the victim, "You're not going anywhere!"

The victim said Hendy hit her head over and over again with a lamp. The victim fought back and hit Hendy with an ice pick that she said was laying around.

She said the bar pulled away from the wall and she took off running wearing only the collar. She said she eventually stopped running when she saw an open door on a neighbor's trailer. She grabbed a woman there and told her what had happened.

Sheriff's deputies and state police officers were summoned to the scene. They took her to the hospital where her injuries were photographed.

"Hendy told me that she had been kidnapping, raping and murdering girls for a year and that Ray had been doing it longer," the victim testified. Hendy also said that they had just done it to a girl named "Angela" and when they get tired of her (victim) they were going to get a 10-year-old girl to train as a sex slave.

Also, according to the victim's testimony, Hendy said they would drug her to make her forget them and what happened, and that they would give her back her clothes and put her on the highway.

Hendy told the victim that they would keep her for a week and another time told her they would keep her for a month, the victim concluded her testimony.

Another victim, known as "Angie" of Truth or Consequences, testified she drove with Ray and Hendy, whom she had met through a friend, Urban Arrey, to their trailer at 513 Bass Road to get a cake mix for her boyfriend's birthday on Feb. 16. "Boy, did I have a party!" she testified.

When she went inside the trailer Ray produced a little box, which Ray wanted to put over her head so no one would hear her scream. He then held a dagger against her throat. He punched her on the mouth and said, "You are being abducted and held against your free will," Angie testified.

Angie asked her friend, Hendy, what was going on but Hendy didn't respond.

Ray chained her up, handcuffed her to a bed and put a chain around her neck. Hendy watched while holding a gun. After removing Angie's clothes they gave her an orange pill. Hendy asked, "One or two pills?" Ray said, "One."

Angie testified she then waited a couple of hours and fell asleep on a single bed next to the living room.

On the second day, Hendy offered her food but she could eat only half of a burrito.

When Ray returned home from work on the third day (he was a mechanic at Elephant Butte Lake State Park), he inserted a wooden object into her rectum.

The prosecutor asked if the victim wanted Ray to do that.

Angie responded, "No sir, I was a virgin."

She testified also that Ray covered her mouth with tape and shocked her with a stun gun.

On the fourth day, Ray gave the victim a bath and took her to the "toy box"—like another little trailer, she testified. Inside, Ray put her on a black table, tied her with red ropes around her waist and feet. After an hour, her tormentors wanted to watch a Stephen King TV special.

They put her on a bed in the toy box and put alligator clips on her nipples and vagina and shocked her for an hour. The device made her shake, she testified. Ray then forced her to perform oral sex on him, which she testified she had never done in her life.

On the fifth day of captivity, the victim said Ray told her to come to the bed and to hug him. He asked Angie if she would be alright.

She said she then tried to make them think that she was their friend "so I could live." Also, she said she was allowed to make phone calls to two different persons. One of them wired money to her on Sunday. Hendy and Angie picked up Angie's money at the Western Union counter in T or C. She said Ray later released her on the freeway where she got a ride.

Angie testified that Hendy had told her she wanted to take a woman named Mela out on a boat to kill her and then keep Mela's 10-year-old daughter as a "love slave." She said she heard both Hendy and Ray say that they had shot and killed somebody in the trailer, but that Ray didn't like blood because it's messy.

"It messed up my head big time. I can't sleep, I'm nervous. I'm thinking that it was my fault. I can't eat and I'm seeing a psychiatrist," Angie testified.

On Sunday, Feb. 20, traveling on Interstate 25, a Luna County Sheriff's Deputy testified he picked up Angie who was flagging down traffic. the deputy, who was off duty and driving a plain pickup truck, said Angie told him she needed to get out of here, that she was going to Albuquerque.

The deputy said that Angie mentioned that he wouldn't believe what had happened; that she just got away from an old pervert and a woman who had her chained like an animal in a trailer.

The deputy testified he asked Angie how would this have happened, and Angie responded that Hendy was her friend, they had been partying together and that "it may have been a drug deal gone bad."

The deputy, an undercover narcotics officer whom the judge shielded from cameras, offered to take Angie to Truth or Consequences to report the incident to police. He said Angie told him that she couldn't make the report because the police are involved.

On the way to Albuquerque, the deputy offered to take Angie to the Socorro State Police office and again she refused and just wanted to be dropped off in Albuquerque.

The deputy said that in terms of credibility he didn't believe Angie's story and thought it was bizarre.

Ray appeared calm and took notes during the proceedings.

The preliminary hearing for Ray was recessed until Friday morning after the Desert Journal's press time.

Hendy's attorney, Xavier Acosta, on Thursday waived the preliminary hearing for Hendy. Her case will go to trial unless she enters into a plea and disposition agreement with the court. She also may be called to testify against Ray.

John Doe identified as Phoenix man

Was David Ray's boss

Desert Journal Staff Report
Friday, April 16, 1999

The body of a John Doe executed and dumped in Elephant Butte Lake nearly a decade ago has been identified finally as Billy Ray Bowers of Phoenix, AZ.

Positive ID of the homicide victim comes on the heels of the investigation into the kidnap/sex torture cases leveled against David Ray, Cindy Hendy and Roy Yancy.

According to KOB-TV Ch. 4 News Thursday night, authorities said Bowers and David Ray had worked together at a Phoenix machine or motors shop (Canal Motors) and perhaps were close friends.

Police are now looking for clues to link the homicide to a suspect. No related charges thus far have been filed against Ray.

"I clearly remember the eerie, gruesome discovery of the badly decomposed body," said Desert Journal editor Bill Johnson. "I was reporting for the Sentinel and photographed the body after boat rangers slowly dragged it to the shore just south of Rock Canyon Marina. The bloated body was wrapped in blue tarpaulin."

"The investigation nine to 10 years ago revealed that John Doe had been shot in the back of the head, wrapped inside the tarp with a boat anchor and dumped in the middle of the lake. The body emerged from the depths after gassing up with the lake's seasonal water warming it up," Johnson said.

"I think its weird the body would be identified after writing about it in an editorial in our 'Hot Spot' column last week. I had no idea that there would be some kind of connection to David Ray," the DJ's editor said.

The Kettle Top area of Elephant Butte Lake is where a John Doe who 10 years later in the wake of the ongoing sexual torture probe at the lake suddenly becomes identified as David Ray's boss, Billy Ray Bowers, at Canal Motors in Phoenix. Bowers' body was wrapped in blue tarp, weighted down with an anchor and a bullet was lodged into his head, execution style.

DJ photo by Bill Johnson

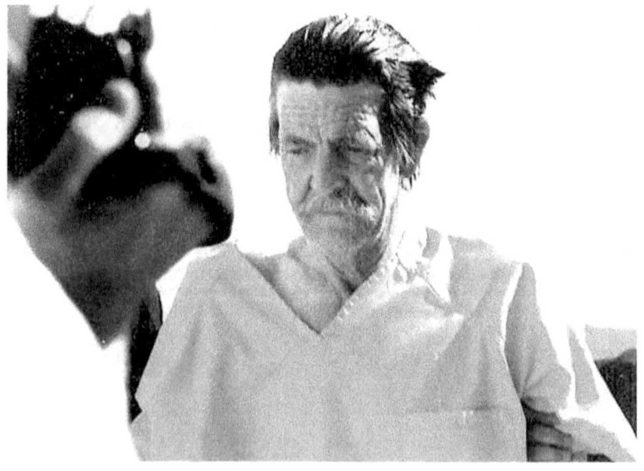

David Ray remains sullen for the cameras in his face.

DJ photo by David Pierre

'Satan's Den' exposed

David P. Ray to stand trial in kidnap, sexual torture case

By Fred Mramor of the Desert Journal
Friday, April 23, 1999

David Parker Ray was bound over for trial in district court last Friday on 25 charges including kidnapping, criminal sexual penetration, aggravated battery and conspiracy.

Ray, 59, along with accomplice Cindy Hendy, 39, is alleged to have abducted and sexually tortured two women at his home at 513 Bass Road at Elephant Butte Lake State Park.

District Judge Neil Mertz ruled after a day and a half of testimony from Ray's victims, investigators and other witnesses there was probable cause for Ray to stand trial for the crimes he allegedly committed in February and March.

A woman who lives one block from Bass Road testified a girl barged into her home at about 3:45 p.m. March 22. The woman said the girl was nude except for a metal collar and chain around her neck, that she was terrified and crying and said, "Please help me, they're trying to get me."

The woman said she called 911 and asked the girl questions until police arrived. The woman's testimony was consistent with testimony given the preceding day by an Albuquerque prostitute.

A Sierra Vista Hospital emergency room nurse testified she received a call from dispatch of a possible rape victim. The nurse said the victim was frantic when she arrived at the ER and said, "Thank you" and "I'm safe" repeatedly.

The nurse described the metal collar and chain the victim wore and abrasions to her wrists and lacerations to her head.

State Police investigator John Briscoe described, with the aid of photos, the contents of Ray's home and of his trailer known as the "toy box."

Briscoe described a device with "prickly things," a table with D rings, an ankle and knee spreader, a "doggie style" bar, and a pulley system with leaded weights designed to stretch the victim's breasts and induce electrical shocks as she struggles.

Briscoe described items including an electrical shocking machine, a cattle prod, human hair stuck to duct tape, a carpet lined coffin-like box equipped with a fan, whips, straps, clamps, padlocks, an "oral stimulator" and other sexual and torture devices.

A blood-stained bed with broken glass on it was found in Ray's home, Briscoe said. Blood spatters were found also on the wall above the bed. Two handguns, a knife, and a badge were found in Ray's home.

Briscoe said he found also medical supplies, surgical gloves and tools, chloroform, ammonia and "poppers."

Briscoe said Ray's toy box was equipped with a gynecological chair mounted on six-foot runners. The chair was equipped with a remote control for various movements sand adjustments. A three and half inch stretcher marked "for vaginal use only" was found also.

Briscoe said he found medical books, a book entitled American Psycho and another entitled "The Dark World of Witches. He said audiotapes and videotapes were found. He did not describe their content.

The toy box was equipped with a video camera and monitor so that the victim could see herself, Briscoe testified. A sign that read "Torture Room" and another that read "Satan's Den" were hung on the toy box's walls.

Also found were drawings of women in bondage. Briscoe said the drawings were in sequence depicting the abduction, removal to another location, and step by step torture of the captive.

Police also found charts with detailed descriptions of the torture that victims were subjected to, and for how long.

Also found were instructions on how to treat captives, stating in part: "new female captive should be bound and moved to the recreation room; she is to be suspended by chains; scissors should be used to remove her clothing; fondle and abuse her breasts; blindfold and verbally abuse; captive is to be suspended at a convenient level; electrically shock victim; use her body aggressively; keep her body suspended and immobilized for two to three hours, and; intensify her fear by telling her she'll be kept as a sex slave."

A final note instructed captors that the shock value of disorientation and abuse will effect docility throughout captivity.

Written instructions on how to handle captives' excuses were found also. "Remember, a woman will say or do anything to get loose. She will kick, bite, scream, lie, threaten, give you sob stories, and tell you of a sick baby or parents.

Cindy Hendy says she's afraid to talk to the press because of what might happen to her.

DJ photo by Bill Johnson

"Never trust a chained captive," the instructions said, and, "if she's worth taking, she's worth keeping."

Cynthia Lea Hendy, Ray's alleged accomplice, was not present at last week's preliminary hearing. She had waived her right to a hearing and entered into a plea agreement with Deputy District Attorney Jim Yontz.

Hendy has pled guilty to five charges including kidnapping, criminal sexual penetration and conspiracy. According to the agreement dated April 6, Cindy Hendy will be subject to a prison term of no less than 12 years and no more than 54 years.

The agreement is subject to Judge Mertz's approval and Hendy's plea may be withdrawn if the court finds any of the agreement's provisions are unacceptable.

In the event of a withdrawal, neither the plea nor any statements arising out of the plea proceedings shall be admissible as evidence against Hendy in any criminal proceedings, the agreement says.

In the case of a third defendant connected to the case, the preliminary hearing for Dennis Roy Yancy in connection with the July 1997 murder of Marie Parker was continued from Thursday (April 22) to

Tuesday, May 25, in the magistrate court in Truth or Consequences.

Last week the Desert Journal exposed Yancy for occult related crimes he committed when he was a teenager in 1987. A confidential informant who knew Yancy then said this week that Yancy and his few satanic buddies told him that they also had wanted to sacrifice a baby.

Ray's daughter Jesse linked to kidnap/sexual torture case

By Bill Johnson of the Desert Journal
Friday, April 30, 1999

The daughter of David Parker Ray has been linked with her father in the alleged kidnapping and sexual torture of a third victim arising from an extensive investigation which authorities say is still in its early stages after five weeks of probing.

The case involving the third victim, identified only as "Kelly" in the criminal complaint filed Monday in magistrate court, is the earliest one so far ending with multiple charges that she was kidnapped and raped repeatedly in Sierra County between July 25 and 28, 1996.

Jessy Ray the day of her arrest at state police headquarters in T or C. DJ photo by David Pierre

David Ray and his accomplice, Cindy Hendy, are accused also of kidnapping and sexually torturing two other victims, a 27-year-old mother of Truth or Consequences and a 22-year-old prostitute of Albuquerque, in February and March this year, respectively, at Ray's residence at 513 Bass Road at Elephant Butte Lake State Park where state police arrested his daughter, Glenda Jean "Jesse" Ray, 32, on Monday morning.

Doug Beldon, special agent in charge of the Federal Bureau of Investigations office in Albuquerque, said more arrests are expected and that the investigation is only in its preliminary stage.

Jesse Ray will spend her 32nd birthday on May 2 in the Dona Ana County Detention Center where she is being kept in lieu of a $1 million cash only bond as continued by Sierra County Magistrate Thomas Pestak at her court arraignment Tuesday in Truth or Consequences.

Pestak told Jesse Ray during her first court appearance that she faces a total of 150 years in prison and a $140,000 fine if convicted on all 12 counts, ranging from first to fourth degree felonies.

David Ray waived his arraignment in magistrate court where identical charges also were filed against him Monday, raising the previous 25 counts already filed against him to a total of 37 counts involving all three of his captive "sex slave" victims.

According to the criminal complaints leveled by state police agent Carrie M. Parbs against the father and daughter, charges related to the "Kelly" case include one count of first degree kidnapping, six counts of first degree criminal sexual penetration, and one count each of second degree conspiracy to commit kidnapping and conspiracy to commit criminal sexual penetration, third degree assault with intent to commit a violent felony and fourth degree criminal sexual contact and conspiracy to commit criminal sexual contact.

Preliminary hearings for David and Jessy Ray related solely to the "Kelly" case have been set for 10 a.m. Tuesday, May 11, in magistrate court.

Jesse Ray's attorney, Billy Blackburn, said his client will plead innocent at the hearing in two weeks. Jesse Ray told news reporters she doesn't know who the mystery victim, Kelly, is.

The district court on April 16 found probably cause to try David Ray on the previously filed 25 felony counts while accomplice Cindy Hendy has struck a plea bargain with the district attorney's office to reduce her 25 charges to the original five charges filed against her in the first case; however, the plea agreement that is still pending the district court's approval exposes Hendy to a prison term of no less than 12 years and no more than 54 years. Hendy was not implicated in the July 1996 "Kelly" case.

The victim Kelly's real name and the affidavit for arrest warrants for both father and daughter were ordered sealed and sequestered by Judge Pestak upon the request of Deputy District Attorney Jim Yontz. District Attorney Ron Lopez has said he's trying to limit pretrial publicity so that the defendants can get a fair trial in Sierra County.

Jesse Ray, bound in shackles, cracked a smile to about five supporters who came to see her during arraignment Tuesday. When Pestak tried to determine whether she qualifies for public defender services, Blackburn protested, saying, "We prefer she fill out the form rather than (verbally) disclose her personal financial matters (before the public in court)."

Pestak ruled Jesse Ray was eligible for the free legal service and waived her $10 application fee.

Blackburn said Jesse Ray wants a jury trial.

"No comment," Jesse Ray said two weeks prior when a Desert Journal reporter approached her for an interview.

After Pestak continued Jesse Ray's bond at $1 million, Blackburn said, "We will continue to adhere to her rights to remain silent."

Judge Pestak then issued a statement to the news media, "Please don't stick microphones in her face!"

One observer said she saw Jesse Ray blow kisses to her friends and heard her tell them, "I love you too," as officers led her from the court for her return trip to the Dona Ana County Jail.

So far, Dennis Roy Yancy, 27, has been charged with the alleged kidnapping and murder of Marie Parker, a mother of two children of Truth or Consequences, in July 1997, although Yancy's wife, Christina, told news reporters that her husband confessed to her after his arrest earlier in April that Jesse Ray forced him to kill Parker under gunpoint while David Ray took pictures of the strangulation death.

A confidential informant told the Desert Journal Wednesday she was at Raymond's Lounge in T or C when Marie Parker walked in crying during the early evening and told her friends, including a bartender and/or a former boyfriend, that she had been raped at the lake (where another informant reported that Marie had been camping with friends, including Jessy Ray and Pablo Nuanes, among others).

The informant said that incident at Raymond's was the last time she saw Marie before she disappeared from the face of the earth during the July 4 holiday two years ago.

The informant said also that Parker supposedly parked her car behind Clay Hines' truck at Bluewaters Saloon in Elephant Butte the night before she came up missing.

"And she supposedly went in and joined a small group of people. She had her purse and car keys. After awhile she said she had to go pick up her kids at her mom's house. Supposedly she put her keys in her ignition and her purse in her car and left. But later when Clay was going to leave, Marie's car was still behind his truck," the informant said.

The informant said people, including the bartenders at Raymond's Lounge, told her that Marie went to Washington state.

Marie Parker's body so far hasn't been found although DA Lopez has said he believes he can successfully prosecute the murder case without it.

A preliminary hearing for Yancy in connection with Parker's murder has been set May 25 in magistrate court.

Since the kidnap-sexual torture case came to light after David Ray's and Cindy Hendy's arrests March 22, several, if not many, local residents have speculated the whereabouts of several other women, one who may be the victim "Kelly" and who were associated with Jesse Ray and/or her acquaintances.

They also are questioning a couple of recent (within the last two or three years) suspicious deaths of people associated within Ray/Hendy/Yancy circles but which have been ruled as either accidental or suicidal.

Several confidential sources close to Jesse Ray said she is a known lesbian and crank (methamphetamine) user and dealer and that they now believe she may have used illicit drugs to lure her and her father's unsuspecting victims to the "toy box" or "Satan's Den"—a small trailer on David Ray's lease lot that was used as his and his accomplices' torture chambers.

<<< >>>

Yancy's brother denies satanic worship

By Fred Mramor of the Desert Journal
Friday, April 30, 1999

"Truth or Consequences is based on rumors. I lived there for many years, they say a lot of things aren't true," said Joshua Norton, adopted brother of Dennis Roy Yancy, suspected kidnapper and murderer of Marie Parker.

Norton said in a telephone interview Tuesday he doesn't know anything about his brother's alleged involvement with satanic worship or the occult, despite documentation by an occult crimes expert in 1987 when Yancy was a teenager. The expert, whose name remains confidential, went on record about Yancy's alleged involvement in occult-related crimes in a story published in the April 16, 1999 issue of the Desert Journal.

"Some people in town claimed that but it was never proven," Norton said. "I asked him (Roy), he said he was never involved in it." Joshua said he believes his brother.

Norton said Yancy had never been strange or dangerous around him or their family and that Yancy had always been there when he needed him.

Norton last saw Yancy three years ago before he (Norton) moved out of state. Norton wouldn't say where. Norton said he heard about the kidnap and murder charges against his brother when a friend from T or C called.

Asked if he thinks Yancy could have murdered Marie Parker, Norton said he wasn't there, that he doesn't know the whole story and just doesn't know if Yancy is involved. He said he knows Roy loved Marie when they were together.

Norton said that he and Parker also were very close. He said Marie liked to go out on weekends and have fun like anyone else but that she wouldn't do anything to endanger herself or her children.

Norton said he wasn't close to Yancy's wife Christina, or Nina, but that she had been a decent person around him and that he doesn't know anything bad about her. He said she always tried to support people.

Norton said he doesn't know David Ray or his daughter, Jesse, or anything about his brother's association with them. Christina Yancy has said Jesse Ray made her husband kidnap and murder Marie Parker.

Norton said he spoke to Yancy a couple of times in the last three years and that he seemed to be the same brother he always knew.

"I love my brother," Joshua said.

<<< >>>

Jessy Ray bound over for trial

Victim Kelly testifies David Ray told her during captivity he was a member of a satanic group that had been watching her and wanted her as a sex toy.

By Fred Mramor of the Desert Journal
Friday, May 14, 1999

Owing to a tell-tale sign in the form of a tattoo, Glenda Jean "Jessy" Ray, 32, will be tried on 12 felony charges including kidnapping, assault, criminal sexual penetration and conspiracy. The same charges have been filed against her father, David Ray.

Magistrate Tom Pestak ruled Tuesday there is sufficient evidence that Ray in July 1996 aided her father in the abduction and sexual assault of a young Truth or Consequences woman to bind Ray over for trial in district court. Both Rays, father and daughter, have pled innocent.

State Police Investigator Keith Rogers testified in Ray's preliminary hearing that a videotape at David Ray's home at Elephant Butte Lake led investigators to Ray's third known victim.

The tape, one of many, was discovered at Ray's home following his arrest in March for the alleged kidnap and sexual torture of an Albuquerque prostitute.

Rogers said the swan tattoo the videotape's apparently unwilling participant wore on her lower right leg led investigators to a 25-year-old woman, identified as Kelly, living in Colorado.

Rogers testified that Kelly told him David Ray tortured her when Rogers telephoned her in Colorado in late April.

Rogers said also Kelly's former mother-in-law reported Kelly's possible abduction and torture by David Ray.

Judy, Kelly's former mother-in-law, testified she called state police in March after hearing news reports about Ray's activities at Elephant Butte.

Judy said her 20-year-old son Patrick and Kelly lived at her (Judy's) Truth or Consequences home for less than two weeks after their marriage in July 1996.

Judy said Kelly's friends, including Jessy Ray, visited Kelly at their home. Judy said Ray came with a woman named Becky—the same Becky who said in a Desert Journal interview she felt lucky she had never fallen victim to her friends, David and Jessy Ray.

Kelly later testified however that Jessy had never been to Judy's home.

Judy said Kelly and Patrick had argued the evening of Wednesday, July 24, 1996, and that Kelly left the house Thursday morning saying she would be back. But Kelly did not return Thursday, Judy said.

Judy said she made phone calls in an effort to find Kelly and Friday filed a missing person's report with T or C Police.

Judy said Kelly returned on a Sunday in a Bronco-like vehicle driven by David Ray. Ray, according to Judy, said he found Kelly wandering on the beach Sunday, that she was dehydrated and that he had given her something to drink.

Judy said Kelly was dirty and had sand in her hair. She testified also that Kelly appeared to be drugged and was incoherent. "Kelly sat there out in space," Judy testified.

The only thing Kelly could remember from the preceding few days was a motorcycle ride Jessy gave her Thursday night, according to Judy's testimony. Judy said David Ray did most of the talking and described the condition he found Kelly in.

Judy said she had heard during Kelly's disappearance that she had been at a bar. Judy testified also that her son had decided by Sunday morning to annul his marriage. Judy said they sent Kelly away with Ray. "We didn't want her to stay," Judy said.

Kelly came again on Monday to see about annulment or divorce papers, Judy testified. She said Kelly was cleaned up and more coherent than she was Sunday.

Judy testified that Cassie, Kelly's and Patrick's friend, was at their home when Kelly returned Sunday. She said Cassie had been at the house on and off since Thursday.

Judy said that after annulment papers were signed Monday, Patrick married Cassie on Wednesday.

Kelly later testified that she had told people she thought Cassie had drugged her so that Cassie could marry Patrick.

Kelly, who appeared to have been crying, testified that memories of her ordeal came to her at various times since the incident occurred. She said she can't remember some things about that weekend.

She said that on Thursday she and her friends went out to different bars and had been at Bluewaters Saloon in Elephant Butte at about 8 p.m.

Kelly said she gave one of her friends a ride home and then was driven back to the saloon by another friend. Kelly said she stayed there with Jessy Ray until 11 or 12. Kelly said Ray then gave her a motorcycle ride to the nearby home of another of Kelly's friends who would give Kelly a ride to her home in T or C, Ray being too drunk to do so.

Kelly said they went instead to Ray's father's home on Bass Road. Kelly said she had been outside the residence on several previous occasions visiting with Jessy and Becky but had never before been inside.

Kelly said she and Jessy went into David Ray's home where she sat on a couch in the living room. She said Jessy went into a back bedroom. Jessy and David came into the living room five to 10 minutes later, Kelly said, and one held a large pocket knife to her throat and the other handcuffed her and put duct tape over her eyes and mouth. She said she couldn't remember who did which.

Kelly said she was strapped naked to what she thinks was a weight-lifting bench and that she had a dog collar around her neck. She said she couldn't remember how she got there but later testified that David led her to a trailer—Ray's infamous toy box.

Kelly said she didn't hear or see Jessy after being blindfolded and that she remembered sometime in the past year that Jessy was not in the toy box.

Kelly's next recollection, which she said came to her about a month after the incident, was of David Ray sexually abusing her. She said Ray, at first unsuccessfully, put a dildo (sexual device) in her vagina. She said he also used his fingers and had rubbed her chest.

When asked by the prosecutor, she said she didn't want that to happen, she didn't want to be kidnapped and she didn't want to stay there. "I just kept telling him I wanted to go home," Kelly testified.

Kelly said she was subjected to at least five episodes of sexual abuse with Ray making at least 30 attempts to insert a dildo in her. She said she remembered at least a year ago that Ray was not completely successful in his sexual abuse of her (he couldn't get his dildos all he way in) and that he ultimately told her she was of no use to him.

Kelly said Ray stayed in the toy box for most of the time she was held but that he left about five times and resumed the sexual assaults when he returned. She said she was allowed to sleep and that she would wake up when Ray returned to the toy box. She said she doesn't remember being fed, given water or allowed to bathe. Kelly said Ray allowed her to pee a couple of times in a port-a-potty by the bench she was strapped to.

She said she remembered the sexual abuse after one month and she remembered the knife after six months. She later testified remembering the knife and dog collar only a couple of months ago and before the FBI contacted her.

Another of her later memories was of Ray saying he was a member of satanic group that had been watching Kelly and wanted her as a sex toy.

Kelly said she had sustained no permanent physical injury but that she couldn't trust anybody the next day and that for six months afterward she would go out only with groups of friends because she had gone somewhere alone with Jessy.

She said she didn't know if she had been drugged, and, contrary to her mother's-in-law testimony, said she was coherent and was aware of what was being said when Ray brought her home Sunday. But she said also her only memory of the incident at that time was the motorcycle ride Jessy gave her Thursday night.

She said she had returned to Judy's home without the watch, ankle bracelet and wedding ring she was wearing Thursday. She said she never recovered the missing items. She said she doesn't remember leaving her mother's-in-law home with Ray on Sunday.

Kelly said she was told of the missing person's report Monday but that she did not call the police to report that she had returned. She said she never told a friend with whom she lived for over a year of her ordeal. She said she didn't tell Patrick about it when they attempted reconciliation in April 1997.

Kelly said she never told anyone until investigators contacted her in April. She said she didn't report it to the police because she couldn't remember what happened. She said she has not seen a doctor or therapist.

Kelly denied hugging or talking with Jessy Ray after the abduction but said she saw Jessy four or five months later but that she didn't remember the circumstances.

New Mexico State Police investigator John Briscoe in his testimony described a photo of a modified weight bench equipped with D-rings and cranks found in a storage shed on David Ray's property. Briscoe said also the port-a-potty Kelly described was found in the toy box.

Audiocassette tapes also were found at Ray's home, Briscoe said.

Defense attorney Bill Blackburn objected to the playing in open court of one such tape, which was dated three years before Kelly's kidnap and assault. Blackburn said the tape was inflammatory, that it was hearsay and that the prosecution cannot link it to Jessy Ray.

Kelly had testified that she doesn't remember a tape being played for her during her captivity.

Prosecutor Jim Yontz argued that the tape describes a female accomplice's part in a captive's torture and is relevant to the conspiracy charges against Ray.

Judge Pestak allowed the tape to be played after Yontz assured him it was not too graphic and wouldn't make anyone sick.

David Ray's recorded voice stated that the material on the tape was for adults only and designed for entertainment purposes.

"Hello, bitch," Ray greeted his victim. "Are you comfortable now? I doubt it." The tape continued, "You're chained, handcuffed, scared and disoriented… listen to the tape, it is very relevant… it was created July 23, 1993, as an advisory tape for female captives from my several years of experience…

"You are here against your will, you don't know what will happen… You will be raped thoroughly and repeatedly in every hole you got… You'll be trained as a sex slave… I don't give a rat's ass if you like it… you might as well get used to it.

"You will be kept as an animal… You'll be fed, watered, and allowed to use the toilet… I'll let you go after two or three months when I'm tired of you…

"My female companion and I are very selective… we prefer girls in early to mid teens, they have small bodies, are easy to control, have tight p---s and make perfect slaves… We also enjoy snatching big titted lesbians from gay bars or we'll snatch anything clean, young and well built…

"You're going to be kept in a hidden slave room stocked to satisfy our fetishes… My lady friend and I find it convenient to keep one or two sex slaves at a time… As the new girl you'll be getting most of the attention… I don't give a flying f--- how you feel about it or about your circumstances… I sure don't respect you: my only interest is that you have an attractive body…

"Your p--- and a-- are going to get a real workout… You'll be forced to eat p--- and suck c---… If you're a young teenybopper, you're going to get an enlightening sex education, you may even like it…

"We're basically like predators, we're always looking… I'm sure you're a great piece of ass but I'll get tired of you eventually… don't want to kill unless it's absolutely necessary… if I'd killed every victim I ever kidnapped, there'd be bodies all over the country…

"As an alternative, you'll be drugged with sodium pentathol and Phenobarbital… you won't remember a f--- thing about this adventure, you'll be dressed and sedated and released on some road," so went the audiotape of narrator David Ray.

Briscoe testified that nine similar tapes were found at Ray's residence. Asked if sodium pentathol and Phenobarbital had been found, Briscoe said numerous pill bottles and syringes were found and are now being tested at the crime lab.

After the prosecution's closing, the judge heard but rejected the defense attorney's arguments to reduce or dismiss some of the 12 charges against Jessy Ray. Ray was returned to the Dona Ana County Jail where she will remain on a $1 million cash only bond awaiting trial in district court.

An experienced court observer questioned Pestak's ruling that the prosecution met its burden in proving probably cause on each of the 12 charges against Jessy Ray. There was no testimony or other evidence that tired her to the actual sexual assaults.

But Deputy District Attorney Yontz said Jessy Ray knew exactly what her father would do with the victim after Jessy brought him Kelly, making Jessy an accessory to the rape.

David Ray waived his right to a preliminary hearing (on the Kelly case) and as such he is bound over for trial in district court.

Another observer said after the hearing she noticed Kate Parker, the mother of murder victim Marie Parker, crying during Kelly's testimony and left the courtroom about five minutes into the playing of the audiotape.

Parker told Channel 13 TV news reporters outside the court building that, besides Dennis Roy Yancy who is accused in Marie's strangulation death in July 1997, she believes both David and Jessy Ray also were involved in her daughter's murder.

Yancy's preliminary hearing is set May 25 in district court. However, no charges thus far have been filed against any co-conspirators in connection with Marie Parker's murder and the criminal information that would reveal the names of suspects other than Yancy—perhaps from one to several suspects or more—has been sealed by the court.

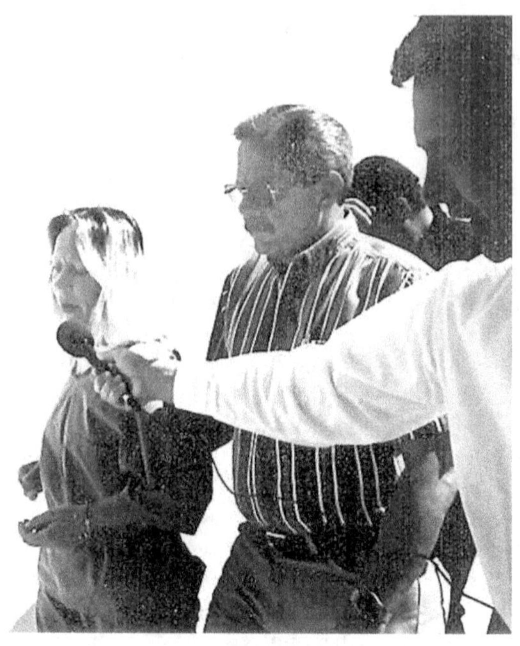

Cindy Hendy alleges David Ray killed some of his victims and dumped them in the lake.

DJ photo by Bill Johnson

Ray killed 14 people, says Hendy

By Bill Johnson of the Desert Journal
Friday, May 14, 1999

Already portrayed as an alleged sex sadist and Satan worshipper, David Parker Ray now faces being labeled a serial killer with the release of court documents Wednesday although no murder charges have been leveled against him thus far into the seven-week plus probe.

Cynthia Lea Hendy, 39, a co-defendant of the kidnapping and sex-torture case in Elephant Butte, told investigators after her arrest in March that Ray said he was involved in killing at least 14 victims. The names of Ray's purported victims were not released in the barrage of search warrants and affidavits that had been sealed under court order.

Ray's attorney, Jeff Rein, told the Albuquerque Journal (May 13 issue) that Ray is maintaining his innocence while Hendy is trying to avoid a near 200-year prison sentence by working out a plea deal that could cut her term to 12 years.

Rein said that in light of the fact that no bodies have been found, Hendy's statement to police should be taken with skepticism. He further told the Albuquerque Journal that Hendy is telling police what they want to hear.

Nonetheless, FBI supervisory special agent Doug Beldon of Albuquerque said the probe is still in its very early stages.

The documents released by the District Attorney's Office this week reveal details of items found, including a coffin-like box with carpet and ventilation holes, a map of Elephant Butte Lake marked with Xs at several locations, identification cards for people who are not known to have had any links with Ray, Hendy or Ray's residence at 513 Bass Road in Elephant Butte, about a hundred videotapes including one that shows a victim strapped down inside Ray's trailer known as the toy box, badges and other law enforcement identification, police radio scanners, possible sound-proofing materials, anatomy books, medical books and a chart depicting methods of sexual torture and bondage, and photographs of women in various stages of bondage.

Hendy in one affidavit described those photographs and told investigators that Ray killed two of the pictured women. In another affidavit, she told police Ray used makeup on his victims so they would photograph properly.

The affidavits also say Hendy gave police information that appears to link to a body discovered floating on Elephant Butte Lake a decade ago.

Beldon said the body belonged to Billy Ray Bowers, who once worked with Ray in Phoenix, AZ. Bowers' body was wrapped in blue tarpaulin with a boat anchor inside the tarp after he was executed—shot in the back of the head, homicide investigators told this reporter in 1989. Bowers' identity was unknown until recently with the ongoing investigation.

According to the affidavits, Hendy told police Ray had admitted to dumping bodies in the water between his residence at Hot Springs Landing and Kettle Top on the east side of Elephant Butte Lake. Ray also allegedly buried or dumped victims at various locations in Sierra County, according to Hendy's statement.

Another affidavit says the age of some photographs indicates the activity had taken place for some time.

<<< >>>

Do victims know they were victims?

By Bill Johnson of the Desert Journal
Friday, May 14, 1999

The Desert Journal caught wind that some of the victims in the David Ray/Cindy Hendy/Jessy Ray/Roy Yancy kidnapping and sexual torture case may not know they were victims.

Courtroom testimony indicates that some, if not many, victims were drugged to sleep and simply cannot remember a thing about their abduction and subsequent torture in David Ray's toy box, also known as Satan's Den from a sign on the wall.

The reason they may be identified as possible victims is because of the photographs and videotapes police seized for evidence. These victims may know nothing about such evidence and police may not readily know the identities of some of these victims.

So, if anyone blacked out for no apparent reason while in the company of any of these four defendants—both Rays (father and daughter), Hendy or Yancy, or their acquaintances and friends—they may have been drugged and then defiled before being released at a place they have no idea how they got there.

But perhaps they'll come to their senses one day and remember when they might have woke up just a second or two to find themselves being sexually abused. Perhaps they may have struggled, said "Stop it!" and then blacked out again. Perhaps meditation or a hypnotist could stir these ghastly memories hidden deep within one's subconscious being.

If prospective victims think they may have been targeted for such abuse and want to really know, perhaps they may want to call the Federal Bureau of Investigations, New Mexico State Police or Crime Stoppers.

Victims may feel ashamed, embarrassed, or confused because somehow they lost control of their bodies or minds to predators who prey upon the weak. But victims shouldn't feel that way because they were deceived, led to believe they had an authentic friendship, by their tormentors—they are the ones to be blamed for their horrible crimes.

And in this case, deception, lies and friendship were used to lure potential victims into the torture chambers where David Ray's indoctrination tapes revealed to victims that they would be drugged and not remember a thing when they leave.

Perhaps forgetfulness on the victim's part may stem from the mere power of suggestion or a threat, inducing fear that something really bad will happen to them or a loved one if they tell; but there could be more victims who simply just don't know. Perhaps they may think it's better to bury the ugly past; but justice won't be served and such an attitude most likely will result in more potential victims—they could be a sister or a close friend.

<<< >>>

Jessy Ray and her friend Cindy browse the tables of the Broken Bend Trading Co. operated by Wild Bill and his team of mules in 1996 three years before her troubles with the law.

<u>DJ file photo by Bill Johnson</u>

Is Jessy Ray a victim?

DA Lopez ponders whether Jessy fell prey to her father's sexual abuse

Desert Journal Staff Report
Friday, May 21, 1999

Did Glenda Jean "Jessy" Ray fall victim to her father with his alleged appetite for sexually torturing young women? Will prosecutors consider that Jessy might have been a victim when they take her to trial for her alleged role in the kidnapping and sexual torture of one of her father's three known victims?

According to District Attorney Ron Lopez, the answer to the second question apparently is no. He said, however, during an interview last Friday that Jessy's possible victimization by her father may be considered at her sentencing, that is if she's convicted of charges.

"She's an adult and knew quite well what was going on," Lopez said. The statement of the victim, Kelly—whom Jessy and David Parker Ray are alleged to have kidnapped and sexually tortured more than three days in July 1996 at Ray's residence in Elephant Butte—indicates there was no apparent coercion of Jessy to commit the alleged crimes, Lopez added.

According to testimony last week, Jessy was said to have delivered Kelly but didn't actually participate along with her father in the sexual torture of Kelly.

Lopez said it would not surprise him if it was true that Jessy Ray had given birth to her father's child. "Anything is possible given the nature of these crimes," Lopez said.

Several sources close to Jessy Ray said Jessy had told them her father, David Ray, is her daughter's father. According to sources, the child is about seven years old and living in Texas.

And according to the Albuquerque Journal, May 14 issue, Jessy had reported to the FBI in 1996 that her father was involved in the sexual torture of women and in the white slave trade, selling his victims as sex slaves to buyers in Mexico.

But according to Doug Beldon, supervisory agent in charge of the FBI office in Albuquerque, the FBI investigated the allegations for a year and found no evidence to substantiate them, the Albuquerque Journal reported.

Friends or supporters of Jessy say they can't believe she's guilty because they found Jessy to be a kind, caring and helpful individual.

Jessy, a mechanic, often helped her friends repair their car problems.

The Desert Journal personally knew Jessy as being concerned with the welfare of animals from an article she had written a couple of years ago about an injured bird she was caring for.

In a Desert Journal "Man-Woman on the Street" interview (June 13, 1997 issue), Jessy was asked, "Why did you come to Truth or Consequences and why are you still here?"

Her answer: "I came here from New Orleans. My dad is a New Mexico State Parks supervisor and I came here awaiting the conclusion of a lawsuit. Then I'll buy property here for renovation and resale. I want to get up a nest egg and start a commercial diving operation in Florida."

Other sources say they knew Jessy to be a lesbian and a crank (methamphetamine) user and dealer.

Dennis Roy Yancy, who is accused of the murder of Marie Parker, allegedly confessed to his wife after his arrest last month that Jessy held Marie at gunpoint while ordering him to strangle her to death and while David Ray photographed the incident in July 1997.

District Attorney Lopez said, however, that he will need more than an accusation against Jessy to tie her to Parker's death. "We need more corroboration. We have no body. It's difficult to make a case against Jessy Ray (in Marie Parker's murder)," Lopez said.

Asked if prominent people or police were involved in the sexual torture case at the lake, Lopez said he had no such knowledge.

Asked whether other arrests are pending, the district attorney said, "If there are more arrests, they will be made as these four cases proceed (against David Ray, his accomplice Cindy Hendy, Jessy Ray, and Roy Yancy). When facing an inevitable prison term for many years, suspects suddenly will save their own skin and will try to minimize their exposure to prison life. As these cases proceed, we will see more things happen," Lopez added.

When asked whether prosecutors were giving credence to Hendy's statement that David Ray had confessed to her that he had killed at least 14 people, including men and women, Lopez said, "The indication, clearly from the evidence, is that we need to spend more time on the investigation. Some other things she (Hendy) has said have been corroborated."

For example, according to the court documents released last week, officers received information that David Ray "was always going out on his boat at all hours. During the search of Ray's residence and the boats at his residence there were found several maps of Elephant Butte Lake. On these maps were spots which were highlighted and which had 'X's' on them. These were primarily in coves in the lake and around the area of Kettle Top... Kettle Top is the dominant feature of the lake one sees when looking out at the lake from Ray's backyard. Information received from co-defendant Hendy indicated that Ray had admitted to disposing of bodies in the water between his residence and Kettle Top."

In the same affidavit for a search warrant, state police said Hendy has stated that Ray described the disposal being done "by cutting open the stomach of the victim so the victim would not rise to the surface."

"Ray had displayed step by step instruction as to how to carry out acts of bondage and torture. It is reasonable that he may have also had additional instruction as to methods of disposal of persons," state police said in the affidavit for a search warrant.

Becky, who has told the Desert Journal she feels lucky for not falling victim to David Ray, whom she called "Dad" despite Ray's protest, said she had told Ray about a former boyfriend who was stalking her.

She said Ray told her while on a boating excursion that the best way to get rid of stalkers is "to open them, put rocks in them, wrap chicken wire around them and drop them to the bottom of the lake." She added that Black Bluffs and Mitchell Point were places they went to while sailing on Elephant Butte Lake.

Profile of an alleged Satanist

FBI's profile of a sex sadist
versus
FBI's unrevealed version

Part 1 of a Four-Part Series

By Bill Johnson of the Desert Journal
Friday, May 21, 1999

While Federal Bureau of Investigations' profilers classify David Parker Ray's deviant behavior as alleged "sexual sadism"—deriving pleasure from sexually torturing others—an underlying, predominant classification can't be told.

At least by the FBI. Or by anyone else in the judicial system seeking justice for the victims of occult-related crimes including kidnap and rape-torture victims Kelly (July 1996), Angie (February 1999) and an Albuquerque prostitute (March 1999) [later revealed as Cynthia] who blew the lid right off the case with her escape.

Satanic worship, believe it or not, is protected by the First Amendment. Occult-related crime, however, lacks constitutional protection although the FBI hits a snag identifying it as such for the public record or the courts. The reason is simple: if the FBI or a prosecutor mentions at trial a defendant's religion or religious belief—be it Satanism or whatever—for being the basis of the commission of a crime, that defendant may end up going free no matter how heinous the crime since the state would have violated his or her civil rights revealing prejudicial or biased information through inadmissible evidence.

Testimony at the preliminary hearing for Glenda Jean "Jessy" Ray—David Ray's daughter who is a co-defendant in the kidnapping and rape charges of one of the three victims of her father known as Kelly—revealed David Ray is a member of a Satanic group.

Ray allegedly told Kelly during her captivity that he is part of a satanic group that has been watching her and wanted her as a sex toy, Kelly testified.

Testimony by police at the preliminary hearing for Cynthia Lea "Cindy" Hendy, an alleged accomplice of David Ray, revealed a sign inside David Ray's torture chambers, that read "Satan's Den" which has also become known as the "toy box" or "play box."

Among more than a thousand items of evidence, police also seized a book on the occult during the execution of a search warrant at Ray's residence in Elephant Butte, according to police testimony.

An admission of belonging to a satanic group and the evidence of several pieces of occult-related paraphernalia may not in themselves prove David Ray is, or was, a Satanist or was engaging in occult-related crimes; his alleged sexual sadism, however, enhances the reason for classifying him as such. And behind closed doors, the FBI profilers have done exactly that but have sealed any reference of a satanic profile of Ray so as not to violate his First Amendment rights and to prevent inadmissible evidence from ruining the prosecution's case, according to reliable confidential sources.

Occult crime can include, but is not limited to: homicide, rape, aggravated assault, battery, burglary, robbery, arson, harassment, animal abuse and destruction of property, according to an independent occult crime expert who spoke only on conditions of anonymity.

No type of satanic worship is illegal in itself. All types of satanic worship are protected by citizens' rights to freedom of religion. The crimes committed by group members, however, are another matter altogether, the expert said.

Two types of occult crime have been identified: ritualistic crime, which is criminal activity that is part of the religious practice, and; occult-inspired crime, which is criminal activity inspired by the individual's religion or religious beliefs.

As a general rule, it is easier to discover occult-inspired crime than ritualistic crime; however, it is sometimes harder to recognize occult-inspired crime as being occult-related.

Ritualistic crimes, because they are an actual part of religious practice and teachings, are always premeditated; occult-inspired crime generally is not.

The thousands of different satanic groups fit roughly into four categories: Satan Worshipers, Splinter Groups, Pseudo-Satanists and Self-styled Satanists; three of which engage in occult crime.

The Church of Satan was founded April 30, 1966, by ex-police photographer Anton Szandor LaVey in San Francisco, CA. It had a membership reaching 25,000 souls.

The church offered satanic baptisms, weddings and funerals. Its influence was felt worldwide and it could boast of mission churches across the country and into Europe.

LaVey, also known as the Black Pope, is the author of the Satanic Bible, which has outsold the Holy Bible on college campuses. Some bookstores in the United States can barely keep the book on their shelves.

Just before Halloween 1987, a joint powers task force in New Mexico had to send an officer to Texas to acquire a copy of the book because every bookstore in New Mexico that carried it was sold out.

During the occult revival of the late 1960s and early '70s, Satanism under LaVey became faddish. LaVey's brand of Satanism is relatively harmless and even attracted stars like Jane Mansfield and Sammy Davis Jr.

When the occult began to lose its popularity in the mid '70s, membership and interest in LaVey's church tapered off. However, his church still exists and LaVey still holds enormous influence over satanic worshippers in the world today.

In the mid-1980s, something sinister began to occur in the occult world that within a few years swept the nation. At the same time that the New Age movement became popular nationwide, a new form of occult practice also began to take shape.

A shockingly high number of juveniles were picking up a new type of satanic worship, with deadly results. Kids were killing in the name of Anton Szandor LaVey.

There are many different types of satanic groups in the United States and abroad today. Some are absolutely harmless. Others are deadly.

In the first category of Satanists, Satan Worshipers refer to members of LaVey's Church of Satan. There is no occult crime associated with this organization. Even so, many people who leave his church later get involved in occult crime.

People of every type and description—both men and women of all ages and professions—belong to the church. No "typical" or "average" member exists and they do not fit into a profile.

Strangely enough, these LaVey Satanists do not believe in Satan as an entity. Their belief is in the power of self. They are basically social Darwinists (the strongest survive). They hold Satan as symbolic of the carnal side, or nature, of man. In essence, LaVey's Satanism is a breed of brutal humanism combined with ritual and dogma.

Their orientation is best summed up in the satanic golden rule: Do unto others as they would do unto you… only do it first! They are oriented to strength; no turning of the other cheek.

LaVey says, "Hate your enemies with a whole heart, and if a man smite you on one cheek, smash him on the other; smite him hip and thigh, for self-preservation is the highest law. He who turns the other cheek is a cowardly dog!"

The Church of Satan is basically harmless from an occult crime point of view. Persons who join however may feel they want more, leave the church and join a more violent category of Satanists. In addition, LaVey's Satanic Bible, which on the whole is also basically harmless, has inspired killings despite its strict prohibition against human or animal sacrifices.

To be continued—A close look at the deadly groups of Satanists next week…

Profile of an alleged Satanist

The Deadly Groups

Part 2 of a Series

By Bill Johnson of the Desert Journal
Friday, May 28, 1999

Accused kidnapper/sexual torturer David Parker Ray, whose alleged behavior has been classified as "sexual sadism" by state police and the FBI, either used Satanism as a means to scare his victims, or he was a practicing Satanist involved in occult-related crimes.

Despite the large volume of evidence—more than a thousand pieces—only a few items linking Ray with satanic activities have been disclosed so far through witnesses' testimony in court or from various hints scattered throughout search warrant affidavits.

Although Ray's alleged criminal behavior may not be a perfect fit for any particular group or category of Satanists, his brand or genre may be self-invented, or self-styled, tailored made to fulfill his alleged predatory, deviant sexual appetite.

Last week, an occult crime expert revealed his research on the relatively harmless Church of Satan, categorized as the first of the four different groups of Satanists. This week, the expert—whose expertise expands beyond research into more practical applications such as the instruction of law enforcement personnel on how to detect, control and prevent occult-related crimes—exposes the deadly groups of Satanists. Who are they? What do they believe? Why are they a threat to society?

The second category of satanic organizations is called Splinter Groups because most of them broke off from the Church of Satan or were created by its former members. For example, The Temple of Set was founded by Michael Aquino in 1975. Set is an Egyptian god whose role is similar to Satan's in western tradition.

Aquino, a former high official in the Church of Satan, had accused Church of Satan founder Anton LaVey of selling high priesthoods to the highest bidder when church funds ran low. Aquino felt a high priesthood should be an earned office, not a bought one.

Aquino wasn't the only one who splintered off. When LaVey announced that high priesthoods were for sale, most of the existing high priests left the church.

Aquino's breed of "intellectual Satanism" is heavily laced with Nazi overtones. Many of the rites of the Temple of Set are very similar to the occult practices of Heinrich Himmler and other members of Adolph Hitler's Third Reich. Himmler ordered the construction of the death camps shortly after he became involved in the black arts.

The Temple of Set and its leader were implicated in a scandal involving the ritualistic abuse of children. Charges did not stick and whether the Temple was involved in illegal activity was a matter of considerable debate and controversy.

Like the Satanic Bible, Aquino's *Crystal Tablet* prohibits human sacrifice and violation results in the offender's immediate expulsion and referral to law enforcement or animal protection authorities.

Not all splinter groups broke off from the Church of Satan and many predate it: for example, the Ophite, Cutus Satanis was founded in 1948. There are hundreds more, and according to the occult crimes expert, the less known they are, the higher the probability for criminal activity taking place.

Pseudo-Satanists, the third category, is the most dangerous but least encountered type of satanic group.

Pseudo-satanic grottos (groups) are highly secretive (the reason they're called pseudo since they don't practice their religion in the open as does the Church of Satan and some splinter groups) and practice a highly sophisticated, complex form of satanic worship that is criminal in nature. Information on these groups comes from members who successfully left the groups, incarcerated criminals abandoned by the groups, child victims and individuals raised by parents who were members, the occult crime expert said.

The grottos are dominated by adult males, the leaders often exhibiting psychopathic behavior traits. Female members are poorly treated and have no authority within the grotto structure.

Many of the grottos have youth auxiliaries, which are controlled by the lower echelon of the adult group, the juvenile members being kept separate from the adult rites.

Pseudo-Satanists not only believe in Satan as an entity, they worship him as a god. They believe that power from Satan increases in proportion to evil committed.

This belief structure results in terrible atrocities and perversions during the rituals. It also over time tends to cause an increase in the violence level of the crimes because with each ritual there is pressure to do something worse than the last time.

Pseudo-satanic groups have existed quietly in this country for a long time. Many groups have been functioning since before the 1930s. They are inter-generational in nature, being run by third and fourth generation Satanists who have been raised in a doctrine of violence. Some groups require members to attend conventional churches as cover. Members may include prominent citizens and business people in the community.

Some groups do not take on new members but the groups, which do accept them require a strict oath of allegiance. The oath is a curse for those members who try to leave.

The orientation of the groups is best summed up by Aleister Crowley's instruction, "Do what thou wilt shall be the whole of the law." Crowley, a turn-of-century occultist, was not a Satanist; he believed he was Satan. He was a serious ceremonial magician and a prolific writer. More than 50 of his books remain in print today. He has a bigger following now than when he was alive.

Crowley is well read by the Pseudo-satanic community and has had a profound effect on it. *In Magick in Theory and Practice*, Crowley said, "For nearly all purposes human sacrifice is best." His records show that he carried out more than 2,400 human sacrifices between 1912 and 1928. [1]

A wealth of evidence indicates Pseudo-Satanists take Crowley very seriously. Crowley recommended a young boy or "perfect innocence and high intelligence" as the ideal sacrifice, but the tastes of Pseudo-Satanists reportedly run from babies through preschool children up to adults, both male and female, and sometimes even rebellious mem-

---

[1] Some of the research on Crowley's activities, including alleged sacrificial homicide, may be biased and inaccurate as it may have originated from his detractors in the Christian community.

bers of their own grottos. Such sacrifices reportedly add up to thousands.

Their rituals are generally sacrificial rites to Satan. One such rite is the modified black mass. Blood is spilled, both to generate magical energy and as an offering to Satan, his devils and his demons. In some cases animals are used; in others, humans are the sacrificial victims.

The reported methodology of pseudo-satanic sacrifice includes the complete and utter destruction of the body. This practice, linked with the highly clandestine nature of the groups who are totally professional about hiding the evidence of their rituals, makes some experts claim there are no human sacrifices.

The question of the existence or number of human sacrifices carried out by Pseudo-Satanists is certainly the single most controversial subject in occult criminology today.

Does the lack of physical evidence mean a crime did not take place? Some believe so; however, the overwhelming volume of specific, detailed reports from law enforcement agencies all over the country strongly suggest that, in fact, human sacrifices are taking place. Additionally, the volume of reports from sources in no way connected indicates the sacrifices—ritualistic homicides—are occurring in large numbers.

All reports of human sacrificial rites include sexual abuse and physical torture or the victim, whether male or female, adult, child, or infant.

The reason for prolonged torture as part of the rite is "magickal." Pseudo-Satanists believe that as the victim—human or animal—suffers, it releases energy. This energy can be trapped with a "magick circle," or in some cases a "magick triangle." Members of the grotto within the circle will absorb this life energy, making them stronger. For this reason alone, Pseudo-Satanists will almost always use a "magickal circle."

The choice of human sacrifice over animal is an obvious one to them: human life energy for themselves, and a more suitable offering to Satan.

Victims vary from drifters, to prostitutes, to street people. Some groups kidnap young children. Some groups place classified ads in newspapers, posing as a couple seeking to adopt a baby. Other groups have "breeders," women who breed babies for the grotto's sacrificial rites.

In a non-supernatural sense, the human sacrifice binds the grotto together. By jointly committing homicide, the group shares a secret. They must trust each other, and yet, at the same time, they have a blackmail power over each other. The result is the group remains cohesive. No one is very likely to report to authorities the atrocities he or she has participated in.

A sacrifice to Satan is a bloody orgy. It may include all forms of rape, as well as mutilation and torture. This includes, while the victim is alive, gouging out the eyeballs, cutting off (or out) sex organs and nipples, cutting out the tongue and other similar actions. Skin may be removed or burnt, and often the victim is forced to ingest blood, urine and feces.

The types and level of torture vary considerably from group to group. In some cases, dismemberment occurs prior to death.

The crimes are committed in such a manner that if reported, they will sound so incredible to the authorities that the reporting party will be discredited. The group leaders depend on this fact to protect their secrecy.

Cannibalism is the final part of the ritual. Death is typically caused by ritual short dagger.

The typical neo-black mass then can be composed of four basic crime elements: kidnapping; multiple rapes in a ritualistic setting; mutilation and dismemberment; ritualistic homicide. These four crimes are known as Level 1 Ritualistic Crime.

Some groups videotape their rituals for limited edition, high-priced snuff films. Acquiring these tapes, if made, is the best chance for prosecution, because the remains of victims are utterly destroyed. This type of murder is called ritualistic homicide, which is part of the belief structure. These are premeditated crimes; killing is part of the group's religion.

Nearly 1.5 million Pseudo-Satanists exist in the United States with some 45,000 grottos ranging in size from 13 to 40 members. Death toll estimates from their human sacrificial rites are estimated to be at least 500 persons per year, according to the occult crime expert.

Human sacrifice is not the only crime Pseudo-Satanists engage in. Another major type of felony crime these groups commit is the ritualistic abuse of children, a Level 2 Ritualistic Crime. Ritualistic abuse is the systematic mental, physical and sexual abuse of young children, typically of preschool age, for the purpose of converting the children to the belief structure.

Although they are the least encountered category of Satanist, for law enforcement Pseudo-Satanists are by far the most dangerous.

To be continued… Next week, a look into the last deadly group—Self-styled Satanists.

<<< >>>

Profile of an alleged Satanist

The fourth deadly group of Satanists

Part 3 of a Series

By Bill Johnson of the Desert Journal
Friday, June 4, 1999

The fourth and last category of Satanists, Self styled Satanists, is the one with which law enforcement personnel will have the most contact. It's the easiest criminal type to locate but the hardest to investigate, according to an occult crimes expert whose research on the subject has been provided exclusively to the Desert Journal.

The expert's research actually began in Truth or Consequences in 1987 when several local teenage boys were believed to have been practicing in the occult and allegedly committed occult-related crimes. Among them was Dennis Roy Yancy, now age 27, according to the expert. Yancy is accused of the strangulation murder of Marie Parker, 22, of Truth or Consequences, in July 1997.

Yancy has waived his rights to a preliminary hearing and now awaits trial on the murder charge in district court.

Police said the case against Yancy is connected to the kidnapping/sexual torture case at Elephant Butte involving three defendants, David Parker Ray, 59, his accomplice Cindy Hendy, 39, and Ray's daughter, Glenda Jean "Jessy" Ray, 32.

More than a thousand pieces of evidence collected at Ray's residence on Bass Road in Elephant Butte suggest also that David Ray was involved in the occult and according to the testimony of one of his three known victims, Kelly, Ray allegedly told her during her captivity he was a member of a satanic group that was watching her and wanted her as a sex toy.

Furthermore, a local pastor who had dabbled in Satanism when he was a teen and has accumulated extensive knowledge on the subject, said Wednesday he found this series of articles on the four different groups of Satanists to be "98 percent accurate." One inaccuracy he cited is that the Temple of Set, identified last week as one of the best known Splinter Groups of Satanists, has no sanctions against human and animal sacrifices, contradicting the expert's assertion that such sacrifices will result in a member's expulsion from the cult and referral to law enforcement for prosecution.

This week, the occult crimes expert exposes juvenile involvement in the occult and the crimes they commit to honor their master, Satan.

Self-styled Satanists are juveniles, mostly male, who have rejected conventional religion and taken up Satanism. Most are high school students, but the trend has moved into middle schools and in some cases even down to the elementary level.

Self-styled Satanists aren't as clandestine as the Pseudo-Satanists, and they lack a specific creed. Each group, self-taught from a variety of sources, has a different ritual structure.

They typically aren't average kids. They are either unpopular, or very bright, or below-average intelligence. In general, juveniles in the middle do not show as great a tendency to get involved. Female juveniles are more rare in Self-styled Satanism, but they do exist.

The only common elements between groups of Self-styled Satanists are belief and orientation. They believe that action equals power, and they are oriented by a desire for power.

The distilled belief is that Satan, whom they regard as an entity and the king of earth, will reward them for evil acts committed. Their concepts of how to worship come from a variety of sources including books, videos, television programs, heavy metal songs, and general population assumptions about satanic worship.

The ritual structure is best described as sacrificial rites and invention. Ironically, the Catholic Church supplies most of the Self-styled satanic rituals since the easiest source of information on satanic worship for juveniles to acquire is books based on records of the Spanish Inquisition. Consequently, juveniles will write pacts to Satan in their own blood and read the Lord's Prayer backwards, something serious Satanists today would never have thought of.

Self-styled rituals include raising demons, rape, homosexual sex, and even some documented human sacrifices. Drug use is heavy and heavy metal music is often played. Animal abuse is common.

A major hallmark of Self-styled Satanism is that the violence level of the practice escalates rapidly. Its creed is anarchy. In Self-styled Satanism, occult-inspired crime is more likely to occur than ritualistic crime. In a sense, to the Self-styled Satanist, all crime is ritualistic. The Self-styled view any anti-establishment activity as paying homage to Satan.

This is the reason Self-styled criminal activity is so diverse. The most common crimes range from threats and harassment to rape and murder. A rapidly spreading crime is "parenticide"—the killing of their parents as a sacrifice to Satan.

Another trait of this category is gang related activity, especially common in metropolitan areas. Sometimes existing gangs take up Self-styled Satanism, usually resulting in a marked increase in the sadism of their criminal activity.

They also will advance quickly to abusing animals with their favorite being cats. But they also torture dogs, goats, cattle, and in some cases wildlife such as deer, elk and antelope. Sacrifice of animals usually entails skinning and/or dismemberment while they're still alive. Certain body parts may be removed, including the head, front or left paws, heart, ears, sex organs and the anus.

Teen suicide also is tied in closely with Self-styled Satanism. The belief is strong in Self-styled circles that suicide is the ultimate honor to Satan and they will be richly rewarded in Hell.

The number of Self-styled Satanists ranges nationwide from 1 percent of the juvenile population in a community to in excess of 50 percent. It is the largest category of Satanists in terms of total numbers. Even a small community could easily have three or four grottos within the juvenile population, each practicing radically different forms of Self-styled Satanism.

They will adopt the trappings of their new religion. They will wear occult symbols openly. Often they dress in black clothing and wear their hair very long or very short.

Self-styled Satanists are sometimes recruited by Pseudo-satanic groups for their youth auxiliaries. When this happens, the youth may suddenly stop displaying the trappings of Satanism. Pseudo-Satanists discourage their youth auxiliaries from being obvious and encourage them to be more clandestine.

To be continued… Coming soon: Analysis and Conclusion.

<<< >>>

Profile of an alleged Satanist

Analysis & Conclusion

Part 4 of a Series

By Bill Johnson of the Desert Journal
Friday, June 11, 1999

While the Federal Bureau of Investigations profilers believe David Parker Ray to be a sexual sadist, evidence and testimony presented so far in the kidnapping/sexual torture case suggests that perhaps occult-related crime also is involved.

Sadistic behavior—deriving pleasure from the torture of others—itself may be a trait commonly found among many practicing Satanists today, according to the independent occult crimes expert, speaking only on condition of anonymity.

The FBI in explaining Ray's alleged deviant, criminal sexual behavior, draws upon behavioral science for its reference source, but shies away from explanations of occult-related activity for obvious reasons mentioned at the beginning of this series: it's not against the law to engage in the practice of Satanism or any religion, and people prosecuted for crimes are treated as responsible individuals rather than as people practicing their unusual religious beliefs. Otherwise, every case with suggestions of ritualistic crime that comes before the court could be tainted with the devil-made-me-do-it defense.

Besides the alleged kidnap and sexual torture of three known victims, the state's case against Ray most likely will not incorporate prosecution aimed at proving any kind of satanic activity. Any evidence submitted as such would be considered inconsequential to the case: the individual will stand trial, not the devil.

Nonetheless, the public eye already has been exposed to clues that perhaps David Ray engaged in occult-related crimes when he kidnapped, raped and tortured his alleged victims. And although the label "serial killer" hangs loosely around prosecution circles, no homicide charges have been leveled against Ray thus far in the three-month-old investigation, said by the FBI to be in its early stages.

In the state's case against David Ray, alleged accomplice Cindy Hendy told investigators that Ray had confessed to her he had been involved in at least 14 homicides of males and females. "In at least one of these situations related by Hendy, officers have been able to verify initial similarities to a body which had previously been discovered in Elephant Butte Lake [a decade ago]," according to state police in a search warrant affidavit filed March 29 in district court.

Hendy also told police, according to the affidavit, that Ray has confessed to her that he has disposed of victims by placing them in Elephant Butte Lake and in one instance describing the disposal being done by "cutting open the stomach of the victim so the victim would not rise to the surface."

In spite of Hendy's statements, which tend to allege that David Ray is some kind of serial killer, no homicide charges have yet been filed against him and Ray has maintained innocence in the state's case against him for the kidnapping and multiple rapes and torture of three victims. "It didn't happen that way," Ray told news reporters after his arrest in late March.

The Federal Bureau of Investigations National Center for Analysis of Violent Crime conducted an initial analysis of documents such as some writings, drawings, journals, photographs, audiotapes and videotapes that were seized by state police. Three experts in the area of sexual sadism said their review of David Ray's activities, including the extensive collection of materials maintained by him, suggests that "he exhibited characteristics of a preferential sex offender, and more specifically a sexual sadist," the affidavit states.

Sadistic fantasies or acts of sexual sadists may involve activities that indicate the dominance of the person over the victim, such as forcing the victim to crawl or keeping the victim in a cage.

"They may also involve restraint, blindfolding, paddling, spanking, whipping, pinching, beating, burning, electrical shocks, rape, cutting, stabbing, strangulation, torture, mutilation or killing. Sadistic sexual fantasies are likely to have been present in childhood. The age of onset of sadistic activities is variable, but common by early adulthood. Sexual sadism is usually chronic," the affidavit states.

Furthermore, when sexual sadism is practiced with non-consenting partners, the activity is likely to be repeated until the person with sexual sadism is apprehended. Some sexual sadists may engage in sadistic acts for many years without the need to increase the potential for inflicting serious physical damage.

Usually, however, the severity of sadistic acts increases over time. "When sexual sadism is severe, especially when it is associated with Antisocial Personality Disorder, [sexual sadists] may seriously injure or kill their victims," the affidavit states.

The FBI's National Center for Analysis of Violent Crime (NCAVC) said that on an investigative level, the presence of "paraphilas" (characterized by recurrent, intense sexual urges, fantasies, or behaviors that involve unusual objects, activities or situations) often means "highly repetitive and predictable behavior focused on specific interests that go beyond the method of operation (MO). The concept of MO—something done by an offender because it works and will help him get away with the crime—is well known to most investigators. An MO is fueled by thought and deliberation. Most offenders change and improve their MO over time and with experience."

For example, one who learns that a body he had dumped into a body of water won't stay on the bottom in spite of a heavy object anchoring it down but instead gasses up and rises to the surface, might improve his MO by cutting open the body to allow the gasses to escape.

"The repetitive patterns of behavior and preferential sex offenders involve the same MO, but are more likely to also involve the less-known concept of sexual ritual. Sexual ritual is the repeated engaging in an act or series of acts in a certain manner because of sexual need; that is, in order to become aroused or gratified, a person must engage in an act in a certain way. In fact, instead of facilitating the crime, it often increases the risk of identification, apprehension and conviction because it causes the offender to make need-driven mistakes. Understanding sexual ritual (need-driven behavior) is the key to investigating preferential sex offenders," the affidavit says.

Kidnapping, rape, torture and homicide also were identified earlier in this series as occult-related or occult-inspired crimes that are committed by members of various satanic cults.

There may be little difference between the definition of sadistic acts and occult-related crime, other than the approach. From a behavioral point of view, there is little doubt that Ray is a sadist, the question remains as to what extent did Ray allegedly engage in any satanic practice or occult-related crime. Did he merely use Satanism as a means to instill fear into his victims' psyche? Or was he a Satanist who believed he would be richly rewarded in Hell for his evil deeds? Or did he actually believe that he was the Beast whose sexual menu must be satisfied by demonic intervention?

...In Conclusion

Answers to these questions may never come out in court; at best, the evidence and testimony to be presented to a fair and impartial jury may only provide some hints or clues in partially explaining the profile of David Parker Ray, who perhaps may go down in history as Sierra County's most infamous criminal if convicted of the alleged crimes in a court of law.

Will Roy Yancy, who confessed to murdering Marie Parker, also admit to the bizarre homicide (mistaken for suicide at the time) of Kenneth Lee Lane at Lane's rock-house apartment in T or C?

DJ file photo

Yancy tied to suspicious death

By Bill Johnson of the Desert Journal
Friday, June 25, 1999

A death ruled as suicide more than three and a half years ago in Truth or Consequences is now being investigated as a possible homicide with spin-off connections to the area's notorious kidnapping and sexual torture case.

The case involving the metallic poisoning death of Kenneth Lee Lane, then 43, is being questioned with possible involvement by Dennis Roy Yancy since he was the only and last person seen at Lane's home before Lane's badly decomposed body was discovered Jan. 1, 1996, at his apartment in the 600 block of West Second Street, according to New Mexico State Police Criminal Agent Norman Rhoades of Las Cruces.

Rhoades said Thursday he has been investigating the case since he received initial reports about it a month ago. "I interviewed one of the neighbors."

Two of Lane's neighbors told the Desert Journal earlier Thursday that they both saw Yancy, 27, of Williamsburg, leaving Lane's apartment at the old rock house from three to five days before Lane's body was found.

Yancy is accused in the strangulation death of Marie Parker, 22, of T or C, in July 1997 and awaits trial on kidnapping and murder charges.

"I, without a doubt, positively identified Yancy. I was still outside. I saw him and another neighbor saw him," said one of Lane's neighbors who spoke only on condition of anonymity.

The neighbor said Lane, a big loner, never had visitors at his apartment expect for the couple or few times that she saw Yancy there. She said Lane after Yancy's visits came outside with Yancy, except this time—the three or four days prior to other neighbors discovering Lane's body—Lane didn't come out with Yancy.

She said Lane always went out on his motorcycle but that it didn't budge after Yancy's last visit there. "His (Lane's) motorcycle was parked right outside my door. This time it was there three to four days and never moved," she said.

She said her other neighbor asked if she had seen Lee and then said that she smelled a foul odor coming through her heater. She said that when Yancy was leaving the last time she said hello to him and he echoed the greeting.

"I did see Jessy (Glenda Ray, also accused in the kidnapping/sexual torture case with her father David Parker Ray) a couple of times in an old car. But I hadn't seen her there for a long time. I last saw Jessy talking outside with Lee about four to five months before they found Lee's body." The neighbor said Agent Rhoades interviewed her.

The other neighbor, who hasn't talked yet with state police investigators, said she was the one who smelled the foul odor coming through her heater. She said that after talking with the other neighbor, her husband, who had a key to Lee's apartment, decided to enter it to check on Lane's welfare. He then called police to report the death, she said.

She said she too saw Yancy leave Lane's apartment four or five days before the gruesome discovery of Lane's body. "The guy who came out of the apartment [in late December 1995] smiled at me," she said, adding that later she realized it was Yancy who was smiling.

She said Lane lived in the apartment about a year and a half. "Lane never had visitors. He was a loner. He left every day on his motorcycle. The only time I saw him was at his mailbox." She added that her observance of Yancy that day outside Lane's apartment was a one time shot for her. "Jessy Ray was there three weeks to a month before that," she said.

"It was weird," the neighbor said. She said T or C Police Detective Priscilla Torrez questioned her and others about Lane's death and told her to go to the police station in three days when autopsy results might be available.

"At first, Detective Torrez said it looked like a murder. Torrez said later on the phone she got reprimanded for what she had told me earlier and that the death was being marked up as a suicide," the neighbor said.

"Everyone I know, we all said this is bullshit. This was a murder," she said.

She said that when Det. Torrez first investigated the death she remarked that "Lane's face was so messed up they couldn't tell whether he was severely beaten or shot. My husband said he (Lane) sure didn't beat himself."

She said she later read in the newspaper that medical investigators ruled Lane's death as metallic poisoning after finding nuts and bolts in his stomach and a door knob lodged in his rectum.

The neighbor said her husband cleaned Lane's apartment and also found blood splatters on the wall. "Lane was into weird stuff. My husband found (inside Lane's apartment) a pentagram (a symbol used in the occult world) and candles on tables and satanic books and other satanic paraphernalia.

She said that when Lane was alive she heard strange music coming through the wall "every once in awhile. Sometimes it was turned up high. He also had all kinds of women's wigs of all hair colors and a cardboard Elvira wearing panties."

She said Lane was living on Social Security income. "The guy next door (Lane) was pretty sick. he didn't bother anyone but he was weird. My husband said he used to do drugs with the former downstairs tenants in their apartment and that Yancy and Jessy Ray often partied once or twice a month there. They did drugs in front of the kids."

She said city police were called to that downstairs apartment regularly and did nothing about their late night parties until 2, 3, 4 or 5 o'clock in the morning and excessive noise. "We called police many times."

She said it might have been possible that Yancy and Lane, who also partied in the downstairs apartment, may have established some kind of drug relationship. She said the people who used to live downstairs left the state and are running from the law.

"I'm looking at it (case)," Agent Rhoades said. He said however it's hard to proceed in a case such as this one since the evidence from back in 1996 was destroyed. "It's also hard to talk to Yancy and Jessy Ray for their confessions as their attorneys will keep them quiet." Nonetheless, Rhoades added, "It looks suspicious to me."

"It'll be real difficult to solve this one. They didn't preserve any evidence. Without evidence, how can you tack it on anybody?" Rhoades asked. "We are looking at it but I don't expect much."

He said that Lane was from Florida and that his body may have been sent there. "If anyone has information, call me," he said. Agent Rhoades may be reached by calling the state police office in Las Cruces at 524-6111.

He said that given the nature of the probe and its limitations, publishing the story should not hinder or jeopardize his investigation. "It could help to publish it," he added.

Lastly, he said, "There appears to be a tie with the David Ray Parker case (involving the kidnapping and sexual torture of three known victims—all young women in their 20s—at Ray's home at Elephant Butte Lake)."

Another confidential source said she told Federal Bureau of Investigations agents early in the spring that Roy Yancy was involved in or somehow tied to the case involving Lane. "And he (Yancy) was arrested two weeks later (in connection with Marie Parker's murder)." [1]

Elephant Butte Lake visitation declines

Many blame fee increase & not David Ray stigma

By David Pierre of the Desert Journal
Friday, July 23, 1999

Elbowroom at Elephant Butte Lake State Park seems to be more plentiful this year because for whatever reason, visitors aren't coming in the droves of years' past.

Speculation as to what is keeping numbers down runs the gamut from user fee increases, elimination of annual camping passes for most New Mexico residents and all non-residents, to weather conditions hampering the appeal of New Mexico's larges lake.

On the surface, at least, the Elephant Butte "trail of torture" rape and possible murder case involving the arrest of four locals isn't an issue among visitors who were interviewed.

The case which Sierra County by storm in March, drawing media from all over the continent, has been quiet since. However, rumors surrounding the centerpiece of the case, David Parker Ray, has the Elephant Butte resident committing the most heinous murder crimes; yet he hasn't been charged with a single murder to date. But many believe the FBI investigators have tight lips concerning findings of the case.

Enjoying the lake with his wife and three children, Dennis Sandoval said the issue hasn't really come up. "To tell you the truth, the murder stuff hasn't really crossed my mind. We enjoy the lake,

[1] End of 11 weekly issues of award-winning investigative series (contest period ended June 30, 1999). The rest is history.

especially when it gets hot. The rate increase (in state park user fees) is a different ball game. I could see why it would bother some people but I don't come to the lake enough, so it doesn't bother me that much."

Others hold an even lighter approach. "I don't know of anybody who's ever said anything about that (sex torture case) or anything for that matter. But the joke is 'Don't drink the water. There's something in it.' The only thing that would keep me away is the number of people. This place is known to get pretty crazy on weekends," said Dale Briscoe, a fireman of Las Cruces who comes to Elephant Butte to enjoy his sailboat every other week in the warmer months.

But those who were interviewed were visiting the lake, still leaving the opinions of absentees in question.

Local merchants have felt the squeeze during the warm months, usually a reliable period for great tourism commerce. "I'd have to check to be exact but our occupancy is down this year," said Pat Knull, manager of the Super 8 motel in nearby Truth or Consequences.

Elephant Butte merchants seem to have reached their limits with the media blitzes. Finding someone willing to talk was a task in itself. "I've been interviewed by I don't know how many reporters. I'm not interested," said one convenience store employee.

"Catch me another day when I'm in interview mode," an owner of an Elephant Butte restaurant said.

Still another business owner at the lake said, "I'm having one of the best summers yet. But I'm not interested in being interviewed, it's just not worth it."

But the city of Elephant Butte's landscape remains peppered with new business construction, indicating the future of commerce in the one-year-old municipality is met with optimism.

However the numbers cannot be ignored. At this time last year, 1.12 million visitors came to New Mexico's most popular state park. Through the second weekend in July this year, just over 900,000 have visited the lake. And they've paid higher rates to enter the park.

The State Parks Division has completely eliminated an $85 annual camping permit that was available to everyone. Now only seniors and handicapped New Mexicans can qualify for a $70 permit that used to be available to them for only $50. All others must now pay $8 or $10 a night, which adds up over a three-day holiday weekend.

EBSP saw nearly 20,000 less people over the Fourth of July weekend but still enjoyed a 12 percent increase in revenue during that holiday.

EBSP Superintendent Rolf Hechler said weather and poor fishing are the major factors for the decline.

"I think the decline in visitation has several factors involved," Hechler said. "Certainly our game fish will have a bearing on that."

"And if you check the weather reports, this spring was a terrible one as far as weather. Easter alone will account for a large margin of that drop—we had, I think, 17,000 (visitors) and we usually get 30,000 or 40,000 or more. The weather was bad; we canceled the sunrise service; we canceled the concert. So it was a bust," Hechler said.

"And those were the two main factors that were involved. I'm not gonna say it was really bad that we lost some visitation at the park. But Elephant Butte had situations where we were reaching capacities. I mean last year on July 4 alone we turned away 5,000 people. It's a concern to me. I think we'll rebound next year," he added.

If one factor stands out as a predominant reason for the decline in park visitation, the rate increase has got to be it.

"It has slowed down because the state park has done a fine job keeping them away. You know they can blame it on the weather or anything they want, but the fact is I've talked to hundreds of people who are incredibly upset with them and when you upset that many people a certain percent of them aren't gonna come back," said Dale Waggy, owner of Guides Choice Bait and Tackle.

Hechler indicated that so many people visiting is hard on the lake and his staff.

Hechler also said the elimination of the camping permit perhaps throws the number of visitors off because the present formula of counting axles and then multiplying that number by 2.75 isn't adequate. "It doesn't account for more people riding in vehicles. because now they have to combine their resources to come to the park. We were trying to eliminate the [huge] number of vehicles that come into the park."

Waggy seemed shocked at the park superintendent's words. "Isn't that an arrogant attitude though—'they'll do it our way or they won't do it all'…? We own the lake, they don't. Rolf doesn't own the lake. We're not his customers, we're his employer. And they've got it backwards. They think we're the customer and we're not. That's very arrogant to suggest such any other scenario."

Waggy also agreed there were other factors. "I think that law enforcement as a whole in this community has verged on harassment. I've watched them right out here. They don't sit still for five minutes and they're pulling someone over. And the car was just going down the road, you can't tell what they're pulling them over for. That's harassment."

"Businesses here are affected. You take 20 percent of the people away from anywhere and it's gonna affect my business," Waggy said.

"I'm so upset that they increased the fees. But to totally eliminate the annual camping permit is ridiculous. I'd like to work with them but it seems like they're trying their darndest to keep people away."

Hechler said he can understand why the rate increase doesn't sit well with some. "We haven't had a rate increase in 10 years. I think the timing was a little off. I think the way they did it was a bit off. Gosh, if it would have been done incrementally throughout the years it wouldn't have been so hard."

Pablo Nuanes at one of T or C's drinking holes during a man on the street interview with the Desert Journal.

DJ file photo by Lucille Benda

Nuanes denies taking a role in Parker's murder

By Bill Johnson of the Desert Journal
Friday, August 13, 1999

Pablo Nuanes, a former Truth or Consequences resident now living in Questa, NM, said Tuesday he had nothing to do with the murder of Marie Parker in July 1997 at Elephant Butte Lake.

Dennis Roy Yancy, 27, of Williamsburg, is the only suspect so far implicated by the state in the murder of Parker, 22, of T or C, who was a mother of two small children and whose body still hasn't been recovered.

Yancy recently pled not guilty in papers filed in the district court of T or C to the charges of murder, kidnapping and conspiracy.

A confidential informant in April told the Desert Journal that she thought Nuanes was involved with several other people in setting up

Parker's assumed death.

"According to that article (published April 16), I sent Marie Parker out there (Elephant Butte Lake) to set up camp. All I asked her to do is to find us a spot so we could set up camp. The Fourth of July party was planned among 14 or 15 so called friends," Nuanes said during his visit to T or C this week.

Nuanes said the party was at the end of what used to be called Jet Boat Cove near the barricaded dead-end of the park road there. "Marie Parker and her children and some of her friends were at the camp site before I arrived," he said.

Nuanes said the last time he saw Parker was at about 5 p.m. July 5, 1997, when she left the camp site to apparently go to Bluewaters Saloon in Elephant Butte. "That's the last time I saw her. A week after that we passed out missing person flyers to find her." Nuanes said he personally distributed the flyers from T or C to the Colorado state border and from T or C to Los Angeles, CA.

The informant has said that Nuanes brandished a weapon to intimidate her when she inquired as to Parker's whereabouts. But Nuanes said he merely was showing off a new bear-skinning knife that he got as a gift. "The only reason I showed it off was because I was proud of it."

"It's on my police record that I never threatened or implied any bodily injury to anyone since 1969. Many people are jealous or envious over my true friendship with lots of other people in town who are my real friends," he said.

Nuanes said that when people mentioned Parker's abrupt disappearance to him he would become upset as anyone who knew her would. "I was in love with the lady but I knew she was too young for me." He added that his love was evident with his flyer distribution effort.

"Every time someone brought up Marie I got upset because of my friendly relationship with her and her two children. People in T or C need to take the time and patience to deal with their own emotions and business," he said.

When asked for a direct response to the informant's story about Nuanes' purported role in Parker's disappearance more than two years ago, Nuanes had this to say: "Dear Mr. or Ms. Informant of the Desert Journal of April 16, 1999: Be informed that God loves you and may he bless you. Signed, Turtle."

On one last note, Nuanes also denied having sold or distributed methamphetamine to anyone as had been alleged by a couple of informants. "I never sold crank in my life," Nuanes said.

<<< >>>

David Ray is hounded by a TV newsman.
DJ photo by Bill Johnson

T or C man says he suspects Ray was up to no good for years

Tracked Ray since 1973 in Arizona and New Mexico

By Bill Johnson of the Desert Journal
Friday, August 20, 1999

A Truth or Consequences man says he believes David Parker Ray was up to no good for years in Arizona and New Mexico, having bumped into and tracked his activities at least once yearly since 1973.

The informant, who spoke only on conditions of anonymity to safeguard his family, said Ray was the leader of a cult that practiced satanic rituals in remote areas of both states. He said he personally knows of one spot in Arizona where Ray and his group set up an altar and possible sacrificed a dog before burying it in a shallow grave. He said he also suspects that people, mostly hitchhikers or transients, whom he met on the road or knew of through conversation, ended up missing because Ray allegedly gave them LSD-laced whiskey to rob them of their belongings or possibly kill them in ritualistic fashion while they were under the influence of the powerful hallucinogenic drug.

The man said he cannot forget a guy like David Ray because he did certain things to attract attention to himself: either he or his female associates, who were known as his "bait" and as his "love slaves," invited park campers and others to their "witches covens"; and Ray often picked up hitchhikers under the informant's watchful eyes. He often left a site where later vultures, flying in circles, would hint at a possible hit. The man said he often wonders whom Ray might have pushed over Arizona's steep canyon walls to plunge to their deaths.

The man said he first noticed Ray in 1973 when Ray was accompanied by a woman who looked a lot like Cindy Hendy. But he's not sure it was her.

The informant said agents of the Federal Bureau of Investigations said they think he drank some of the whiskey after he told them in May that God told him to help them in their case against Ray and his accomplice, including Hendy, in the multiple kidnapping and sexual torture case at Ray's residence at Elephant Butte Lake State Park. The case came to light in late March with the escape of one of their victims.

"I first ran into this group in Albuquerque in 1973," the informant said. "I left my career as an electrician in Chicago, picked up a hitchhiker in Missouri and dropped him off near a commune in the downtown Albuquerque area. Ray and a chick were getting into a car, put something on its roof and before they left they stopped, turned around and watched this guy get out of my car. He (hitchhiker) went into the commune.

"I then went to Tijuana, Mexico, and five days later to the Grand Canyon where I saw Ray again. The woman (Hendy look alike) came by the campground to say there would be a witches' coven tonight. I was with four or five people. I asked, 'When?' and she said after the dance that night at Yavapai Bar. After she left a guy asked, 'Does anyone know where to get some pot?'

"Later we walked to the host's at the camp site and he said Ray had two love slaves and Ray spiked whiskey with a hundred hits of LSD (per bottle). I went to the dance and saw Ray sitting there. The next night we heard about roadblocks and about a girl who was raped. I went on the main road east to the Painted Desert and I saw Ray taking people into the woods.

He recalled that the Flagstaff newspaper published a picture of the dead girl. "Her parents were politicians from back east," he added.

"I also heard they left another (girl's) body by Rye, AZ, in the summer of 1977. They found a strangled body by the side of the road. Bodies were intended to be found," he said.

He said the same woman (Hendy look alike) also was at Verde Hot Springs in 1977 or so and invited a half dozen guys to a witches' coven there. "She said David Ray was having a witches' coven and that he was the leader. The next morning she complained she had a rape victim (a girl).

"They (Ray and his group) were at a lower campground and we were at the upper one. She said the victim was hysterical. I heard them move stones to obscure their site of ritual practices. She said David was probably in Phoenix (having left already) laughing because the rest of his group was still there where roadblocks had been set up. She spoke about having to go back to Oregon to get refingerprinted because they (authorities) screwed up the first set.

"When I was at the back side of Roosevelt Lake in 1981 looking for jojoba beans, Ray cut me off. I went up the road as he came out of it. I went up it only a quarter of a mile where there was the only water (in the vicinity). It was a steep area under trees where someone had cut a flat trench. It looked like an altar. There was a grave in front of it. It was fresh and had no stones. That's where I found the dog only three inches deep," the informant said.

He said about two weeks later after he checked out the dog's grave, about nine cars showed up and after an hour or two they left in different directions as if to invite more campers to their covens.

They found two bodies there that week. One death was ruled from natural causes. The body was found by the site where the vultures were (circling). I don't know the cause of death of the other one. It was in mid-August 1981," he said.

"I left the area and in about a month I saw him again in high country cruising around campers. I set up camp at Roosevelt Lake to do some trapping. About 15 cars went across the lake to an Indian holy site with lots of Indian ruins. One guy dropped off another guy at my campsite and he wanted to sleep in my car and dig up the ruins at night, but I said no. He never took his eyes off that site.

"A month later I camped across the lake within a quarter of a mile from where these cars gathered. A cowboy asked me why I dug up ruins but I wasn't, I was out trapping. Five U.S. Forest Service agents patrolled and camped in the area to do surveillance on me. They dressed like hunters in brand new clothes. Later they questioned us in Globe and we didn't tell them about the guy. The guy who did it (dug up ruins) was in jail 30 days for stealing a bottle of whiskey. I think he was an accomplice (of Ray's)."

He added that in 1981 at Roosevelt Lake he also saw the woman (Hendy look alike) throw clothes into a dumpster and then throw another set of clothes into another dumpster. He said he also saw her and Ray wash out a tarp in the Salt River the same year.

He said that during the couple of years that he trapped and prospected he ran into Ray many times, especially during holidays. He marked on the Arizona map highlighted lines on roads and "Xs" on four spots where he believes Ray might have killed people. "There are two more possibly in the Grand Canyon," he added.

The informant said that after he moved to a remote area of Roosevelt Lake, AZ, in 1981 he kept seeing vultures across the lake. "I saw flocks of vultures numerous times in a six-week period above the cliffs. I also saw David Ray in the area more than five times and once he invited my girlfriend at the time to a witches' coven."

"I saw Ray almost every year since 1973 somewhere out in the woods and he moved here (Sierra County) at about the same time I did in 1982. In 1987 (or so) I saw him and a woman at Elephant Butte Lake when they (authorities) found a couple of bodies in the lake. I also saw him pass a whiskey bottle in Flagstaff in 1974 or 1975. He had two twin blondes he always traveled with and who I called his Swedish love slaves.

"He had connections all the way to California. He gave rides to a lot of people. He took hitchhikers or foreign tourists or backpackers to Death Valley or the north rim of the Grand Canyon. He always comes back to check on them.

"I think someone was feeding the vultures about five miles from Roosevelt Lake. They (Ray and his group) cruised from campsite to campsite on one side of the lake randomly inviting people to the witches' covens. I heard the woman (Hendy look alike) mention such covens that evening at Pinto Creek or on the other side of the lake in a remote area.

"Ray got people to think they'd have sex with his love slaves. He used the women as bait. I saw her (Cindy look alike) at the Christopher Creek Bar in 1981 and one guy was hitting on her while Ray looked on. Someone ended up missing and the bar was the last place he was seen. Ten miles south of the bar a fisherman ended up missing. A lot of pot growers at Verde River ended up missing too. I believe it was mass homicide."

"One guy invited me to his camp site at Fossil Creek and told me he had a sign across his tent that read, 'Caution, guard snake inside.' When I got there no one was around. I looked inside the tent and all I saw was a sleeping bag and a whiskey bottle three quarters full. I think it was spiked with LSD. I never saw him again. I think someone later took his tent."

"The people who told me about the whiskey and acid looked for Ray to learn his trade. I figure Ray used this concoction to hijack and rob people and/or possibly to strangle them to death."

The informant then pulled out a photo of the Roosevelt Lake area showing a cliff overhang over a steep canyon wall. "I thought Ray was dumping bodies off this cliff but I never got a chance to check it out." On the photo, he also pointed out the site of the witches' coven (or altar) was where the water disappeared.

"My ex-girlfriend did craft shows of her bead work. I also worked at Kole's Ranch near Christopher Creek below Mogollon Ridge. Ray once gave me a ride from Globe to Superior and he offered me whiskey. I didn't take a drink. I also saw him go by Union Hall several times with hitchhikers. I also watched him picking up hitchhikers in front of a motel in Globe. He tried to give me a ride too."

"After Labor Day 1991 I took a trip to Supai on the Havasupai Indian Reservation and on the way back I was heading into Wickenburg where I saw vultures four or five miles off a dirt road with steep cliffs. I saw Ray come out on the road. He turned up the road and also watched the vultures. Once vultures land no one knows what's going on. I went to the rest area and saw Ray changing directions back to Wickenburg."

The informant said Ray always had a big station wagon, like a Buick, usually gray or silver and at one time light green. The back seat was always down with a tarp over a bunch of camping gear or "it could have been loot from backpackers," the informant said.

"One time I saw him on a back road going from Beaverhead to Horse Springs, NM. I've seen him cruise Datil, one time outside Quemado and Fence Lake, NM. I saw Ray near Peyson, AZ, at a popular swimming hole checking out young girls in their bathing suits."

"I probably saw Ray at least 25 times since 1973. I've seen Ray passing whiskey to Indians in Flagstaff and Holbrook, AZ, and in Gallup, NM," the informant said.

"I spoke to him once in 1987 or 1988 at the Cuchillo Bar. He told me I could come home with him (to Elephant Butte) that night and that he could get me a job at the state park service (state park where Ray worked). He told me he had a soundproof room (at his home) but he didn't explain why."

The informant said he also had learned that a tri-state task force consisting of the states of New Mexico, Arizona and either California or Texas, was formed to solve a rash of murders.

He said the circumstances and coincidences involving his travels and bumping into Ray all of these years were the reason he decided to try to give information to the FBI three months ago. He said the FBI told him to give them a call if he should remember where any bodies could be found. He said he now remembers through photographs he had taken and is now ready to talk to the FBI again.

Mertz to hear cases of David & Jessy Ray, high court rules

Judge Neil Mertz

By Fred Mramor of the Desert Journal
Friday, August 27, 1999

Seventh Judicial District Judge Neil Mertz will preside over David Parker Ray's and Glenda Jean "Jessy" Ray's infamous Elephant Butte kidnapping and sexual torture trials, according to Wednesday's ruling by the New Mexico Supreme Court.

Defense attorney Billy Blackburn's 17-page petition to excuse Mertz from Jessy Ray's trial was denied, according to the court clerk's office.

The high court ruled also that Mertz must decide whether both the father and his daughter will be tried separately or together.

Both Rays are accused in the kidnapping and sexual assault of a young Truth or Consequences woman in July 1996. Ray additionally is charged along with Cindy Hendy in similar incidents involving two other women at his home in Elephant Butte earlier this year.

<<< >>>

Burlap bag of human remains not connected to EB torture case

By Bill Johnson of the Desert Journal
Friday, September 24, 1999

A burlap bag containing human remains found last summer at Elephant Butte Lake by a fisherman has not been connected to the multiple kidnapping-sexual torture case at the lake, according to state police Tuesday.

Sgt. Rick Anglada, speaking on behalf of the New Mexico State Police Public Information Office but who works in the Internal Affairs Investigative Office, said he wouldn't be too quick to speculate that the body parts had anything to do with the case involving co-defendants David Parker Ray, Cindy Hendy, Glenda "Jessy" Ray and Dennis Roy Yancy, or murder victim Marie Parker, as has been reported in various news media around the state.

"I can't say at this time there is anything to connect these remains to the kidnapping-sexual torture case at the lake. I can't say how long the bag was in the lake before it was found. These things just haven't been determined yet. We just have nothing to connect the two cases," Sgt. Anglada said.

He said the body parts only recently were confirmed to have belonged to a human. Gender, age, and other characteristics have not yet been determined of the victim, Anglada said.

He said also that no decision has been made yet whether the remains will be tested for DNA, an examination that may done by the FBI rather than by the NMSP.

<<< >>>

Trials likely to be moved for both Rays

By Fred Mramor of the Desert Journal
Friday, October 8, 1999

District Judge Neil Mertz probably will grant a change of venue in the trials of kidnap and sexual torture defendants David Parker Ray and his daughter Glenda Jean "Jessy" Ray.

Mertz in an elimination of standards hearing last Monday instructed David Ray's attorney, Jeff Rein, and Jessy Ray's attorney,

Billy Blackburn, to submit nominations for suitable venues. Mertz cautioned the attorneys not to expect him to be familiar with court dockets and schedules around New Mexico.

Seventh Judicial Assistant District Attorney Jim Yontz did not resist the change of venue.

Rein in his affidavit and motion for change of venue filed Tuesday states, "The nature and extent of publicity in this case has been pervasive, persistent, lurid, and extensive. Reporters from local, regional, state, national and international media services have covered this story."

"Each court appearance is reported in the T or C newspapers, the Albuquerque papers and released on the Associated Press wire service. Members of law enforcement and the District Attorney conducted daily press conferences in the early stages of the investigation. The case was quickly labeled the 'David Ray Sex Torture Case'," Rein's affidavit said.

"Updates about the status of Mr. Ray's case or the progress of the cases of each of the co-defendants are a common feature of the local news. A fourth individual, Roy Yancy, has been linked through the press to Mr. Ray. The police have publicly, and consistently, speculated that bodies have been buried in the Elephant Butte area and that Mr. Ray is responsible. Although no bodies have been found, the hysteria and lurid curiosity of the press and public in this case have not dimmed," Rein said.

Rein's affidavit states that the stories and the number of media sources presenting the stories have combined to create such public excitement or local prejudice in Sierra County's and the Seventh Judicial District's jury pool that Ray cannot receive a fair trial in the four-county district.

Rein in his motion did not say where in New Mexico his client would get a fair trial. Blackburn during Monday's motions said he has no particular venue in mind at this time.

The trial dates for both Rays have not been set and are not expected to be scheduled until the distant future.

At Monday's motion hearing, Judge Mertz ruled the elimination of standards as requested by the prosecution.

"The state is seeking to gather from the defendants items for comparison. Ray's counsel is holding out forever and the state needs to eliminate David Ray as a possible defendant," Yontz said. The evidence collected includes thousands of items from David Ray's Elephant Butte residence and his "toy box."

Blackburn had no objection. He said it may be exculpatory for his client. He said items seized were from early 1999 when Jessy Ray was not living in the area.

Rein was concerned about the collection of DNA evidence. Yontz said the state might elect to take gum or saliva samples from David Ray.

Judge Mertz said he could sign the order as long as the gathering is not more invasive than the prosecution has said, otherwise, the defense must be notified.

Rein said the DNA tests will require independent analysis given that the FBI lab has been less than competent.

Yancy rape victim talks

But says Yancy may not have killed Marie Parker: Identifies murder witness; Site of body may be known

By Bill Johnson of the Desert Journal
Friday, November 12, 1999

A Truth or Consequences woman said Tuesday that Dennis Roy Yancy, 27, raped her in October 1998 but may not have murdered Marie Parker in July 1997.

She said a possible witness to Marie Parker's death told her after the Elephant Butte Lake kidnapping and sexual torture case came to light last March that he was with Parker in a tent at the lake when he saw Pablo Nuanes strangle the young mother of two children to death.

Nuanes already denied any involvement in Parker's murder during an August interview at the Desert Journal. He said Parker apparently disappeared from the face of the earth after the Fourth of July party at the lake. He said the last time he saw her was at 5 p.m. July 5, 1997, when she left the campsite apparently to go to Bluewaters Salon in Elephant Butte.

"I was in love with the lady but I knew she was too young for me," Nuanes had told this reporter.

Another confidential informant had told the Desert Journal that after Parker's disappearance she inquired of Marie's whereabouts but Nuanes became irritable and at one time brandished a weapon, as though he was threatening or intimidating her over her persistence.

"The only reason I showed it (a new bear skinning knife he says he got as a gift) off was because I was proud of it," Nuanes said.

However, the woman who alleges Yancy raped her, said Bob Ashley told her and another witness, whose identity she refuses to reveal, that he (Ashley) was there when Nuanes killed Parker.

"There were only Pablo, Bob and Marie in the tent. Yancy was not there. Marie was heavily on drugs," said the woman who spoke only on conditions of anonymity, fearing retaliation for speaking to the press.

"That's why Roy (Yancy) couldn't find a body," the woman said, referring to Yancy's failed attempt to lead police to Parker's body at a burial site in a remote area of the desert west of the lake after his arrest in April on the murder charge. "He didn't know where she was."

"Why Yancy (allegedly) admitted to killing her, I don't know," the woman said.

She said also that a woman with whom Ashley had sexual relations told her last weekend that she knows where Marie's body is.

"I didn't want to know and told her to tell me no more," she said. "She was having sex with Bob Ashley and apparently he told her where Marie's body is."

The woman in question said she couldn't comment on any statement she may have made of the whereabouts of Parker's body. During an interview Wednesday morning at the Desert Journal, she said she would have to first get authorization from her attorney or someone else to speak, and if she talks it will be on only conditions of anonymity.

"I do fear for my life," said the woman who so far has declined to tell her story about Ashley's statement to police. "If they got Bob and know what he told me, I think my life is in danger. Bob was my friend for six years. I was the one he called every time he went to jail. He knows I'm the one who would help him," the woman said.

"I think Bob Ashley is dead... He knew too much. He gets drunk and talks too much."

She said Ashley left the Cutter area in May, went to a rehabilitation center in Seattle, WA, and was last heard from, as she understands it, in June.

"Why did Yancy take the rap (in an alleged confession to police)? Maybe he was scared for his life... He may be in jail for protective custody," she said.

According to Yancy's wife, Christina, Yancy told her after his arrest that he was forced under gunpoint to strangle Parker to death. He said Glenda Jean "Jessy" Ray held the gun to his head while Jessy's father, David Parker Ray, took photographs of the incident. Yancy however is the only suspect accused so far in the Parker murder case.

"When [the woman] came to see me and told me she knew where the body was, that verified Bob's story," the woman said. "I will be willing to take a lie detector test on anything I say," she added. She also signed a paper saying her statements are true to the best of her knowledge.

Despite her statement, which tends to clear Yancy of wrongdoing in the Parker case, she said he raped her (the informant, not Parker) after drugging her near the river in Truth or Consequences 13 months ago.

She had fallen unconscious during the incident but a couple of hypnotic sessions, conducted by contract through the Desert Journal, helped her recall some details, but not all of them.

Dorothy Marietta, a natural health practitioner and hypnotic therapist of the Natural Life Center in Bosque Farms, said she suspects that something happened to the victim.

The woman said she had known Yancy as a friend four to five months prior to the rape incident and that they never had a sexual relationship before then.

She said she was at her sister's home in T or C where several people were drinking beers in the front yard and where Yancy and Jessy Ray just had a big fight or argument. After the fight, Yancy asked the woman (the informant, not Jessy) if she wanted to go to the river to look at the stars. "I was willing to go."

"Yancy was very obsessed with me—just being there all the time. He didn't want me to do any drugs. We were just basically friends," she said.

After reaching a spot along the river, Yancy got on top of the van and helped her get on top too. "After I sat down everything got weird. I was losing my thoughts. I got confused," she said, adding that they took a six pack of beer to drink at the river. She said after Yancy pulled her up, she started drinking a beer that Yancy had opened. She said she suspects Yancy drugged her. "Shortly after, he stared me in the eyes to where I couldn't move."

"I remember laying down to look at the stars. He tried to have sex with me. I didn't want him to." Weeping, she said, "There was a struggle and he was very rough… Things were violent. He was holding my arms down, restraining me with some kind of weights to hold my arms together on top of my head. He pulled my pants halfway down and became angry and real crazy—something I've never seen before. He penetrated me a little bit but I was fighting like hell."

She said ropes were also on top of the van but she didn't know how they got up there. "It was instant chaos. I was not cooperating. I was scared. I would never expect that from him—trying to have sex with me."

At some point, she said she lost consciousness and woke up on a bed covered in white sheets in a room with "bright, bright lights." The ceiling was white, everything was white, very bright. I didn't see the light but it was very bright and hurting my eyes."

She said Yancy sat two feet away from her. "It seemed a long time and I couldn't move my eyes from him, so I couldn't look around. For hours it seemed his eyes were in my eyes, like they were attached. I couldn't move a muscle. I tried. There was nothing I could do except look into Roy's eyes. I never saw eyes like that. I couldn't move a finger."

She said Yancy said nothing, didn't touch her and he seemed scared, and that she heard nothing and later she woke up at her sister's house and that she still could hardly move.

"I don't remember getting in the van (at the river) to go there. I can't remember anything before waking up in the bright room."

She said her hands had swollen up and she noticed that her rings were missing from her fingers. "He (apparently) got my jewelry off. I don't remember if he cut them off but they were cut off," she said.

"I saw him the next day or two and the rings were laying on his floorboard. He said he had to cut the rings off because my hand swelled up real bad. He had wire cutters on top of the van. I didn't see him put the ropes [there] too."

She said she asked him about the other night and he told her he tried to have sex with her and that she went crazy.

She said that after she arrived at her sister's home where she was living at the time, Yancy didn't leave and sat on the couch the rest of the night. She said that before the incident Yancy was there morning, noon and night and slept in his van outside her sister's home.

"I didn't remember any of this until the story broke (about the kidnapping/sex torture case at the lake)," she said.

She said that about two years ago she tested positive for hepatitis C. "A month later (after the rape incident) I ran into Roy and he told me he got a test at the health office and found out he too has hepatitis C. It came from me," she said.

"I think Jessy (Ray) saved my life. I think that's why they (Roy and Jessy) fought. I think she was trying to protect me… My sister never saw me like that in my life. I couldn't function for quite awhile."

"Jessy, the last time I saw her before her arrest in April, couldn't look at me. I just thought she had family problems. She didn't lift her face up and didn't look into my eyes," she said.

She said Yancy later came to her house and wanted a place to stay. "He was really, really drunk. I told him he had to leave."

She said she saw him one more time before the story broke. "He came to my house, walked in, asked how my husband was, and saw a male friend there. He turned around and left quickly."

"I never expected anything like this to happen from Roy. I could expect it of others. Yancy was always polite and didn't do drugs. I didn't know his wife. I knew he was married. I just never saw eyes like that. It was the eyes that freaked me out more than anything else."

"His eyes were very bright, bright, bright—very green, green, green, like evil. The times [with him] on the van and in the bed (in the brightly lit room) were the only times I saw this evil. His personality changed right after his fight with Jessy. He (Yancy) had a lot of girlfriends. His nickname was Toy Boy Roy."

She said she still doesn't know where the room is that Yancy took her but is certain that it wasn't David Ray's infamous toy box at his Elephant Butte Lake residence where he allegedly took his kidnapped victims and sexually tortured them.

"I was really, really scared, but I'm a tough chick. I felt like I died a little bit. I don't feel right mentally. I was pretty strong but I didn't beat it—the sex, the restraints. I want to remember so bad I can't. I want to remember everything—where the room was and why I was gone so long (up to seven hours from the time they went to the river and returned to her sister's home at about 3 a.m.)

"I just feel like something terrible happened. I know it in my soul. I think Roy was an evil person. I think he didn't want me to do drugs at the time because the drugs he would give me could kill me."

She said she believes the nature of the rape incident was "satanic".

She said she told her husband what happened after the hypnotic sessions in August. "Now he's divorcing me because he thinks I was cheating on him, but I didn't. I was raped."

She showed a letter written last week on Nov. 3 in which her husband told her he filled out the divorce papers.

Hendy wants to change plea to not guilty

By Fred Mramor
Friday, November 12, 1999

Cindy Hendy, a defendant in the Elephant Butte sex torture case, wishes to change her plea from guilty to not guilty, according to Assistant District Attorney Jim Yontz.

Yontz said Monday no formal motion has been made but that Hendy's attorney, Carmen Garza, told him of Hendy's desire to change her plea.

Asked for comment, Yontz said, "It will be up to the court. If the court accepts her not guilty plea, we'll take her to trial. If not, we'll go to sentencing."

Yontz said there has been no word about trial dates or a change of venue for any of the four defendants in the case but that a motions' hearing, which he described as "housekeeping," has been set for the district court in T or C Nov. 18.

Yontz said he hopes the hearing will include a change of venue and that things are otherwise quiet for the time being.

Trials set for both Rays

Court grants videotaped depositions at David Ray's trial

By Fred Mramor of the Desert Journal
Friday, November 19, 1999

David Parker Ray will stand trial for his alleged crimes in the Elephant Butte kidnapping/sex torture case on March 28 in Tierra Amarilla as ordered Thursday afternoon by District Judge Neil Mertz.

Ray's daughter, Glenda Jean "Jessy" Ray, will be tried July 10 in Gallup for her alleged role in the case, according to the judge's order changing venue and notice of setting for jury trial.

David Ray's trial is set for 9 a.m. in the Rio Arriba County Courthouse in northern New Mexico while daughter Jessy's trial is scheduled for 9 a.m. in the McKinley County Courthouse.

Jessy Ray's attorney, Bill Blackburn of Albuquerque, had requested a change of venue because of "saturated" pretrial publicity in the news media of Sierra County, Las Cruces/El Paso and Albuquerque areas.

In another late breaking development Thursday morning, Judge Mertz granted the state's motion to offer videotaped depositions from witnesses in David Ray's case in a district court hearing in Truth or Consequences.

Assistant District Attorney Jim Yontz said the state received information that witnesses Donald and Darlene Breech may move from the area and may be unavailable to testify in court against Ray.

Yontz said the Breech's taped testimony will be important as it will describe alleged victim Cynthia's appearance and what she said when she entered their home after escaping Ray's Elephant Butte torture chambers last March.

Yontz said the state will still try to secure the Breech's appearance but that it may be virtually impossible if they relocate.

Ray's attorney Jeff Rein did not object to Yontz's motion. Rein did however say the state's acknowledgement of its duty to preserve items containing DNA evidence is unsatisfactory.

Yontz after the hearing said a hearing regarding DNA evidence will probably be held in mid-January. Pretrial hearings will continue to be set in Sierra County or elsewhere at the convenience of the court, according to Judge Mertz's order.

David Ray, 59, is accused in criminal complaints of the kidnapping, rape and torture of three women from 1996 to March this year. Daughter Jessy is accused in one of those cases involving victim Kelly in 1996.

Present in the courtroom Thursday morning were Marie Parker's mother, Kate, and Pablo Nuanes.

<<< >>>

Yancy sentenced to 20 years

Desert Journal Staff Report
Friday, December 10, 1999

Dennis Roy Yancy, 28, of Williamsburg, was sentenced to 20 years in state prison after pleading guilty to the murder of Marie Parker, 22, of Truth or Consequences, more than two years ago.

According to the plea and disposition agreement filed Dec. 2, Yancy agreed to plead guilty to second degree murder and conspiracy for the incident occurring between July 5 and 9, 1997, in Sierra County. He entered the plea and was sentenced by District Judge Neil P. Mertz during a hearing in Socorro.

Mertz sentenced Yancy to serve two 15-year terms to run consecutively for a total of 30 years, followed by two years parole, but suspended 10 years of the sentence provided that Yancy complete five years of probation; otherwise, he could be exposed to a 32-year term in a state correctional facility. The two years of parole will run concurrent with probation, the judge ordered.

As part of the agreement, other charges that may arise from Parker's death will be dismissed, according to the agreement.

In addition, Yancy agrees to pay restitution as determined by the probation and parole department.

According to prosecutors, Yancy has agreed to cooperate with them by testifying in the infamous Elephant Butte Lake kidnapping and sexual torture cases pending against three defendants: David Parker Ray, Ray's daughter Glenda Jean "Jessy" Ray, and Cindy Hendy.

Dismembered calf found at middle school

By David Pierre of the Desert Journal
Friday, December 10, 1999

Last Saturday evening a young cow was found dismembered at the Truth or Consequences Middle School.

Players of the school's basketball team returning from a tournament found the calf at about midnight, The team's coach, Kelly Lee, after seeing the calf, called 911 authorities immediately.

When the kids first told me, I thought, 'Oh no, it's going to be some kind of ritual thing with an altar or something.' But when I saw it my first reaction was that it was a bad prank," Lee said, dispelling an appearance of satanic sacrifice.

The calf was found in three black plastic garbage bags in the breezeway near the school office. The animal probably was brought to the school by a vehicle because droplets of blood led to the bags from the loading zone driveway in front of the school.

"There's a lot of ways to go about charging a crime like this," said Livestock Inspector Olin Lynch who was one of the first on the scene. "We have criminal damage to property. But when I find out whose calf it was we'll have larceny of livestock which is a third degree felony," added Lynch.

The head, shoulders and ribs were found in one bag. Another bag contained the four legs of the animal with the limbs sticking out of the top.

Yet another bag was apparently partially torn open with the innards spilling out, according to T or C Animal Control Officer Roy Schoenradt who was dispatched to the scene at 12:20 a.m. "The calf was torn up. It was different, it was definitely out of the ordinary," he said.

"The livestock inspector wasn't ruling out Satanism, but said he had been called upon in the past on actual Satanic sacrifices and said this was different.

"You never can tell for sure. I'm not going to even speculate," Lynch said.

Once the killing was examined and photographed by Lynch the dead calf was taken to a remote area and buried.

"They used a bone saw," said Lynch, who said the killing wasn't consistent with satanic sacrifices because the genitals of the animal were intact.

"Other Satanic cases almost always have the sex organs removed and are part of the ritual. The sex organs were intact in this case," Lynch said.

The calf apparently just had been killed. "According to the police it was still steaming when they arrived," Lynch said.

Other than who would do such a dastardly act and why, one thing still remains a mystery. Lynch could not identify a cause of death. "I don't know how they killed him. There was no gunshot wound and his neck wasn't cut," he said.

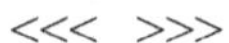

David Ray seeks separate trials for each of three alleged victims

Cindy Hendy's motion to withdraw plea rejected

By Fred Mramor of the Desert Journal
Friday, January 21, 2000

Seventh Judicial District Judge Neil Mertz will take under advisement a motion to sever counts against Elephant Butte kidnap/sex torture suspect David Parker Ray.

Defense attorney Jeff Rein argued in a hearing last Friday that it would be too prejudicial to try Ray on charges including kidnapping, assault and criminal sexual penetration relating to three victims—Cynthia, Angie and Kelly—in a single trial.

Prosecuting attorney Jim Yontz opposed defense's motion to sever the counts against Ray. "They're yelling about all the publicity in the case and yet they want to try those separately. If we have one trial the publicity is going to go crazy and it will be harder to find a jury the next time," Yontz said in an interview Wednesday.

Barring an order to sever counts, Ray's trial has been set for March 28 in Tierra Amarilla.

Judge Mertz in a hearing Tuesday denied Ray's suspected accomplice Cindy Hendy's motion to withdraw her guilty plea made last April to five charges and plead not guilty to all charges.

Yontz said he opposed defense attorney Carmen Garza's motion because, "She (Hendy) made a knowing and voluntary plea of guilty and we don't see a need for another trial (in addition to Ray's and his daughter Jessy's)."

Yontz added that Hendy probably will be sentenced in four to six weeks and will face a minimum of 12 years and a maximum of 54 years in state prison.

<<< >>>

Hendy's sentencing postponed

By Fred Mramor of the Desert Journal
Friday, April 21, 2000

Sentencing for Cindy Hendy, alleged accomplice of Elephant Butte kidnap/sex torture suspect David Parker Ray, scheduled for Thursday, April 20, in district court has been postponed.

Judge Neil Mertz granted defense attorney Carmen Garza's motion to continue as she had to appear in court in Dona Ana County for another of her clients, Jason Desnoyers.

When sentenced Hendy will face a term of imprisonment from 12 to 54 years having pled guilty to charges including kidnapping and criminal sexual penetration involving two victims more than a year ago at Ray's residence at Elephant Butte Lake.

Hendy sentenced to 36 years in prison

Says she'll appeal guilty verdict; Meanwhile, victim Angie dies

By Fred Mramor of the Desert Journal
Friday, May 12, 2000

Cindy Hendy received sentences totaling 36 years in prison in district court Thursday for her participation with David Parker Ray in the kidnap and sexual torture of two young women in Elephant Butte last year.

Hendy had pled guilty to two counts of kidnapping, two charges of criminal sexual penetration and one count of conspiracy to kidnap.

Judge Neil Mertz handed down consecutive and concurrent terms for the five offenses resulting in a final sentence of 36 years. Hendy, 40, will be eligible for parole after 18 years.

The sentence may not satisfy one of Hendy's known victims, an Albuquerque prostitute named Cynthia, who asked the judge to sentence Hendy to 54 years in prison, the maximum term he could have imposed.

Cynthia, choking back tears, said, "You'll get out of prison someday, but I have to live with this for the rest of my life."

Cynthia's grandmother, Rosa, will have to rely on a higher court for justice. "I hope Satan has a place for you in hell and that you burn there forever," Cynthia's grandmother said.

Hendy's other victim, Angie Montano, formerly of Truth or Consequences, was denied the opportunity to see punishment meted out to her tormentor. Angie died Sunday in an Albuquerque hospital, reportedly of pneumonia and heart failure.

District Attorney Ron Lopez and Assistant DA Jim Yontz said Angie's death will not affect prosecution of the alleged mastermind in the sex torture case, David Ray, as they will use her testimony from Ray's preliminary hearing last year in his upcoming trial.

The cell door has not closed on Cindy Hendy and she may not yet escape punishment in this world. Judge Mertz informed Hendy that while appeal in this case as she had requested withdrawal of her guilty plea on grounds that she did not have the capacity to understand the consequences of her plea. The judge had denied her motion to withdraw the guilty plea.

Hendy said she will appeal as the sheriff escorted her from the courtroom.

<<< >>>

Jury selection for David Ray's retrial to begin late November

By Fred Mramor of the Desert Journal
Friday, November 3, 2000

Jury selection for Elephant Butte kidnap and sexual torture suspect David Parker Ray's retrial will begin Nov. 27 in Estancia, NM, 7th Judicial District Attorney Ron Lopez said this week.

Ray's June trial in Tierra Amarilla resulted in a hung jury when 10 jurors returned a verdict of guilty but two jurors found Ray not guilty of abducting and torturing a young Truth or Consequences woman named Kelly in 1996.

Lopez said he will never understand the two female jurors' reasoning, which he said was not based on evidence or logic. He said the two jurors said they couldn't tell from Ray's videotapes—containing pictures only and no sound—if the alleged victim was crying or laughing.

Lopez said he thinks only a confession would have convinced them of Ray's guilt.

Lopez said also one of the two jurors may have resented the alleged victim because of her resemblance to a woman the juror's husband had recently left her for.

Lopez further revealed prosecutors learned after jurors had begun their deliberations, and when it was too late to do anything about, that the two jurors, along with an alternative, had discussed the case with each other when carpooling to the trial from Espanola. The district attorney said however he can't prove it and it wouldn't be worth pursuing the matter if he could.

Ray's retrial is scheduled to begin Jan. 2 or 3 in Estancia after a jury has been selected before the Christmas holiday.

Lopez said he will be happy to be back in the 7th Judicial District as it was difficult to prosecute in Tierra Amarilla where motel rooms served as offices, and evidence and witnesses had to be transported some 330 miles from the Elephant Butte area.

Lopez is optimistic about his second crack at Ray because he said prosecutors have done extremely well in Estancia in past cases and because he hopes the court will reconsider its rulings barring certain evidence from the first trial.

Two more trials will be scheduled next year for Ray's alleged kidnap and sexual torture of two other young women. But prosecutors will consider whether to bring those cases to trial if they succeed in convicting Ray in Kelly's case, Lopez said.

The district attorney said it may not be worth taxpayers' money to try Ray on the other cases if he is convicted in Kelly's case and spends the rest of his life in prison. Lopez said also he may not want to put another of Ray's alleged victims, a former Albuquerque prostitute, through the ordeal of testifying against Ray unnecessarily.

A third alleged victim, Angie, has died since Ray's arrest but Lopez said her testimony will be extracted from Ray's pretrial hearing if that case is brought to trial.

Jessy Ray, daughter of David Ray, will be tried separately in Gallup in late March for her part in Kelly's alleged abduction and torture.

<<< >>>

Judge Mertz dies Thursday

David Ray's case on hold

By Bill Johnson of the Desert Journal
Friday, December 1, 2000

District Judge Neil P. Mertz of Socorro died Thursday morning, Nov. 30, in Socorro during a two-day recess of the infamous David Ray trial.

"It came as a great surprise and everyone is in shock around here," said Seventh Judicial District Court Administrator Kim Padilla when reached at her Socorro office late Thursday morning only a few hours after Judge Mertz's death at age 57.

"He was a great boss. It's a major loss to his staff, his community and definitely throughout the Seventh Judicial District (which consists of all of Catron, Sierra, Socorro and Torrance Counties, comprising one of the biggest judicial districts geographically in the country, if not the biggest)," Padilla said.

The death of Mertz casts shadows on the likelihood of the immediate continuance of the trial for accused kidnapper and rapist David Parker Ray in the notorious Elephant Butte sexual torture case involving three victims, all young women. Jury selection for the Ray trial began Monday, Nov. 27, in Estancia, Padilla said.

The selection of jurors was postponed early Wednesday, however, after Ray's defense attorney, Lee McMillan, came down with a severe case of laryngitis, Padilla said.

The trial for Ray was expected to reconvene today (Friday, Dec. 1), and Judge Mertz was to hear cases in Socorro on Thursday, Padilla said.

But Judge Mertz died at Socorro General Hospital after his heart had stopped Thursday morning and the ambulance was taking him from his Socorro home to the hospital apparently as the result of a heart attack, Padilla said.

"They tried to stabilize (or revive) him in the emergency room, but instead they pronounced him dead," she said.

Asked about the status of the David Ray case and how it will be handled without Mertz as presiding judge, Padilla said she just didn't know. "It obviously won't be Judge Mertz," she said, adding that the decision for a restart and appointment of a new judge to the case will be up to the defense and prosecuting attorneys involved in the case.

Mertz was appointed to the bench by Governor Gary Johnson after the New Mexico Legislature created a third judgeship for the judicial district.

He began his stint as district judge on March 26, 1996. Then in 1998 Mertz faced Truth or Consequences attorney Anthony Filosa in the November general election and managed to keep his seat on the bench.

Before serving as district judge, Mertz had worked for District Attorney Ron Lopez in Socorro and before then he had a private law practice, also in Socorro 75 miles of Truth or Consequences.

Mertz is survived by his wife, Paula, a son and daughter, his parents of Texas and possibly a brother and sister, Padilla said.

Funeral arrangements were pending as of press time Thursday at Steadman-Hall Funeral Home in Socorro.

Retrial for David Ray set April 2 in Estancia

His daughter's trial postponed in trail of sex torture case

By Fred Mramor of the Desert Journal
Friday, March 9, 2001

Prosecutors will have a second chance to convict David Parker Ray in a retrial scheduled to begin April 2 in Estancia, NM, Seventh Judicial District Attorney Clint Wellborn said this week.

Ray's first trial for the kidnap and sexual torture of Kelly Van Cleave, a young Truth or Consequences woman, at Ray's Elephant Butte home in July 1996 ended in a hung jury last July in Tierra Amarilla.

Charges against Ray included kidnap, assault, criminal sexual penetration and conspiracy.

Jury selection for Ray's retrial had begun last November but was suspended when Judge Neil Mertz died. Judge Kevin Sweazea of Socorro has since been appointed to replace Mertz and will preside at Ray's retrial.

Depending on the outcome of the retrial, prosecutors may or may not proceed against Ray in cases involving two other alleged victims, Cynthia Vigil and Angie Montano, the district attorney said.

Vigil's dramatic escape from Ray's Bass Road home at Elephant Butte Lake in March 1999 led to Ray's arrest and to evidence of his crimes against three young women.

Vigil, then an Albuquerque prostitute, reportedly has left her former occupation and has married and had a child.

Montano, a reputed local party girl, died from pneumonia and heart failure last year.

Having entered into a plea agreement with prosecutors, Ray's alleged accomplice and girlfriend Cindy Hendy received a 36-year prison sentence for her participation in Vigil's and Montano's kidnap and sexual torture. She will be eligible for parole after 18 years in prison.

The trial of another of Ray's alleged accomplices, Glenda Jean "Jessy" Ray—his daughter—was scheduled to begin on March 26, but has been postponed and will be scheduled for a later date, the district attorney said.

Ray convicted in EB Lake sex-torture case

Two more kidnap-rape cases to go to trial

By Fred Mramor of the Desert Journal
Friday, April 20, 2001

After a five-day trial and five hours of deliberations, an Estancia, NM jury Monday night found David Parker Ray guilty on all of 12 charges including kidnapping, criminal sexual penetration, assault and conspiracy in the sexual torture of a young Truth or Consequences woman at Ray's Elephant Butte Lake home in 1996.

Assistant District Attorney Jim Yontz on Tuesday said Ray faces a basic sentence of 135 years but as prosecutors will seek aggravated status on the charges, Ray could be sentenced to 180 years in prison.

Ray reportedly will appeal his conviction "all the way to the supreme court" but Yontz said he has never seen a criminal case and conviction where the defense didn't file an appeal. Yontz said it's standard practice.

Ray was tried in Tierra Amarilla, NM, in the same case but the trial ended last July in a hung jury forcing the retrial in Estancia.

Yontz said he may have won his conviction the second time around in part because he presented evidence somewhat differently than in the first trial and because a different judge, Kevin Sweazea, presided over the retrial. Yontz shared credit for his win with Claire Harwell whom he described as an exceptional co-prosecutor.

Yontz added that the first trial may have been lost owing to two jurors whom he heard had been involved with "the bondage and discipline world." Yontz said the two jurors may not have been sure that Ray's victim wasn't a willing participant.

Yontz said Kelly, Ray's victim, is happy with the outcome of the retrial and that he is happy for her more than for anything else.

But Kelly will have to relive her nightmare ordeal at least once more in the trial of Ray's co-defendant and daughter, Glenda Jean "Jessy" Ray. Jessy Ray's trial had been set for March 19 this year but was postponed after the death of Judge Neil Mertz. A new trial date has not yet been scheduled.

Trials have been set for David Ray for June 11 and Aug. 8 this year in two other cases of kidnapping and sexual torture involving a former Albuquerque prostitute, Cynthia Vigil, and another local young woman, Angie Montano.

Montano died from heart failure and pneumonia since charges were brought against Ray in the three cases. Prosecutors will rely in part on testimony she presented in one of Ray's preliminary hearings.

In the meantime, the district court ordered David Ray to undergo a 60-day pre-sentencing evaluation at the Department of Corrections facility in Los Lunas. Yontz said he anticipates the sentencing hearing on Ray's recent convictions will be held after Ray's second trial.

David Ray accepts plea agreement

Also will plea guilty to federal white slavery charges, says prosecutor

By Fred Mramor of the Desert Journal
Friday, July 6, 2001

David Parker Ray on Monday pled guilty to charges of first degree felony kidnapping and conspiracy to commit kidnapping and to second degree felony criminal sexual penetration in the abduction and sexual torture of former Albuquerque prostitute Cynthia Vigil at Ray's Elephant Butte Lake home in March 1999.

Having been convicted in April on similar charges in a case involving Kelly Van Cleave, a young woman formerly of Truth or Consequences, Ray will face up to 238 years in state prison in a sentencing hearing expected to be held in September or October, possibly in Truth or Consequences.

The plea agreement precludes Ray from appeal or other motions in the Van Cleave case, Assistant District Attorney Jim Yontz said Tuesday.

Ray did not tell Yontz why he accepted the agreement but Yontz said one incentive may be that state prosecutors will not oppose Ray doing federal time before serving his sentences in state prison.

Yontz said Ray will plead guilty to two felony counts under a federal White Slavery Act, essentially for holding persons for involuntary servitude.

Yontz said the federal charges have not been filed but that he had suggested them to recognize the work the FBI has done in the case and to justify their continued investigation and evaluation.

After Ray is sentenced on federal charges, Yontz said it will be up to the Federal Bureau of Prisons as to whether they will accept him. Yontz said the Bureau may not accept Ray at first but may take him after he has spent a hundred or so years in state prison.

As to why Ray would prefer to spend the rest of his life in federal rather than state custody, Yontz said he doesn't know that Ray would be more comfortable as a guest of the federal government but that he may have a longer life expectancy as some of his victim's relatives are serving sentences in state prison.

As part of Ray's plea agreement, charges will be dismissed in a case involving another of Ray's known victims, Angie Montano, who died of pneumonia and heart failure after testifying against Ray in a pre-trial hearing.

Yontz said Montano's mother recognizes that as Ray was convicted in Van Cleave's case and has pled guilty in Vigil's case, only a paper conviction would be gained in prosecuting her daughter's case. Angie's mother will however have the opportunity to be heard at Ray's sentencing hearing.

Dismissing charges in the Montano case will of course spare the state the expense of further prosecution and witnesses the ordeal of testifying, Yontz added.

David Ray's plea agreement in no way involves his daughter, Jessy Ray, who will either face trial or enter into her own plea agreement for her alleged participation in the abduction and sexual torture of Kelly Van Cleave, Yontz said. Jessy Ray's trial date has not yet been scheduled.

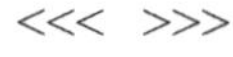

David Parker Ray (right) and his attorney Lee McMillan (left) listen to the expert testimony of FBI agent Mary Ellen O'Toole who testified Thursday afternoon that criminal sexual sadists, such as Ray, generally aren't treatable. Ray will never walk the streets again—District Judge Kevin Sweazea sentenced him to more than two centuries in prison during Ray's sentencing hearing in Truth or Consequences.

DJ Photo by Bill Johnson

David Ray gets 224 years

Victims weep, 'criminal' sexual sadist looks on

By Fred Mramor of the Desert Journal
Friday, September 21, 2001

David Parker Ray was sentenced to 224 years in prison at a hearing in Truth or Consequences Thursday having been convicted of numerous offenses involving the abduction and sexual torture of three young women at his Elephant Butte Lake home.

Ray was convicted earlier this year for his crimes against Kelly Van Cleave, formerly of Truth or Consequences, in July 1996. He later pled guilty to charges involving two other victims, the late Angie Montano of T or C and Cynthia Vigil of Albuquerque, in 1999.

Defense attorney Lee McMillan unsuccessfully argued for withdrawal of Ray's plea agreement on grounds that Ray was incompetent to make informed decisions while under the influence of numerous medications.

Prosecutor Jim Yontz argued, and Judge Kevin Sweazea agreed, that Ray had been alert, responsive, conversant, able to assist in his own defense and aware of what was going on during his trials and other proceedings. Judge Sweazea denied Ray's motion to withdraw his plea.

Mary Ellen O'Toole, Federal Bureau of Investigation agent in Virginia and the FBI's foremost expert in the field of investigating criminal sexual sadism, testified Thursday that examination of Ray's home, the trailer he had converted into his infamous "toy box" and the sexual paraphernalia and drawings found there suggest that Ray is a "criminal sexual sadist."

She said Ray's toy box and custom equipment were extremely impressive in terms of sexual sadism, their potential lethality and the time, money and effort it took to keep them a secret.

O'Toole said there is no known therapy for Ray's paraphilia (psycho-sexual disorder) and that its corresponding behavior can be stopped only by apprehension.

Ray's victims made their statements to the court and to Ray before the judge pronounced sentence. Kelly (Van Cleave) Garrett who earlier was crying and holding hands with Cynthia Vigil in the courtroom, said she wants Ray to live a for long time and suffer in prison.

She said the sick pervert will find no friends in prison and she hopes he will be controlled and used in the same manner that she and

Ray's other victims had. Garrett said however she is not a victim but a survivor.

Loretta Romero, Angie Montano's mother, said her daughter had a good heart but had lost all respect, lost her smile, lost everything because of David Ray. Mrs. Romero said she is here for Angie and her two little boys whose lives Ray had ruined. Mrs. Romero said she feels sorry for David Ray, that she forgives him and that her (now deceased) daughter would forgive him. But Angie's mother said she never will forget.

Less forgiving was Cynthia Vigil's grandmother, Bertha Vigil. Mrs. Vigil told Ray he is a poor excuse for a human being and asked him how he would like it if she did to his daughter what he had done to Cynthia.

Bertha Vigil said her granddaughter has nightmares every night and that Ray had ruined not only her life but her whole family's.

Cynthia's grandmother said she prays Ray will suffer every day for the rest of his life. "Satan has a place for you. I hope you burn in hell forever," Mrs. Vigil said.

"I bare scars outside and inside that will never heal," Cynthia Vigil said. She said no punishment is equal to the agony she has suffered. Vigil said she is afraid of being tied down and helpless, afraid of the dark and of going out alone. Cynthia Vigil, crying, said she hopes David Ray will spend the rest of his life inside four walls and suffer the way he made her suffer.

Attorney General Patricia Madrid said she was pleased to be at Ray's sentencing for the people of New Mexico. Madrid said Ray's behavior was worse than that of any animal.

She said he had reduced his victims to abject terror and thought of them not as human beings but as "packages." She said Ray posed a particular danger to the community by enlisting young accomplices.

Madrid pleaded with the court to impose the maximum penalty on David Ray saying that the community cannot risk any chance of his freedom. The attorney general said Ray's plans and his illustrated manual make it clear that he will torture another human being.

Prosecutor Jim Yontz said it has been two and a half years since he has thought about what he would say today. Yontz said Ray's crimes differ only in scope but not in nature from events in the world outside this small community.

Yontz said Ray had picked the wrong victims. He commended Angie Montano, Cynthia Vigil and Kelly Garrett for their courage and fortitude. Yontz warned the court that if Ray is ever released, he will offend before he gets home.

"This monster should never be allowed to walk the streets again," Yontz said. "There should be no light at the end of the tunnel and he should realize that a cell will be his home for the rest of his life and that he will leave only in a box."

Defense attorney Lee McMillan conceded that his effort to have Ray's sentence reduced to 173 years suspended with only ten years actual prison time, which he called a "death sentence," was like rearranging deck chairs on the Titanic.

McMillan pleaded that the term paraphilia does not do justice to the disease his client has suffered. Ray, 61, has "successfully" resisted his disease for almost 50 years and has made efforts to reform himself while in protective custody, McMillan argued.

Ray, who seemed to be in good spirits during his sentencing hearing and unmoved while his victims cried, said he is having a hard time expressing himself. Despite his handicap as a public speaker, Ray told the court that no one but his attorney had heard his side. Ray said many lies and distortions have been told in his case.

Ray commended the late Judge Neil Mertz who, according to Ray, said Ray never had a fair chance at a fair trial in Sierra County and therefore moved his trial to Tierra Amarilla. That trial, Ray reminded the court, ended in a hung jury.

The defiant Ray criticized Judge Sweazea—who would soon sentence Ray—for moving the second trial to a venue conveniently near the judge's home. Ray criticized also Patricia Madrid for taking the credit and being on camera after another prosecutor, Claire Harwell, who could not be present for Ray's sentencing, had done all the work.

Ray said he had entered into a plea agreement to get his daughter released. Ray's daughter, Glenda Jean "Jessy" Ray, was Ray's accomplice in the abduction and sexual torture of Kelly Van Cleave.

Jessy Ray, recently released from custody with five years probation, sat with spectators, victims and the press during her father's sentencing hearing.

Ray argued, as his attorney had, that his judgment had been impaired by the numerous medications he had been taking. He said he never really knew what was going on when he was allowed only 15 minutes on the phone with his attorney each week while in custody.

Ray said he had lost everything following his arrest including his home, all other material assets and his health.

Ray said the two and a half years in confinement since his arrest has allowed him to reflect, read his Bible and "get right with God." Ray said he has put his life in His hands and that he can't change the past but can only be sorry.

Judge Sweazea was not swayed by Ray's statements. Sweazea said that after sitting through Ray's trials and hearing the compelling testimony of Kelly Garrettt and Cynthia Vigil, he can only imagine the horrors they suffered.

Sweazea said that though the purposes of sentencing are incapacitation, punishment and the possibility of rehabilitation, in Ray's case the primary purpose will be incapacitation so that no one else will suffer at his hands.

Sweazea noted Ray's extensive preparations demonstrated the extensive time, effort and money that went into his horrific crimes.

For his crimes against Kelly Van Cleave, Judge Sweazea sentenced David Parker Ray to nine years for kidnapping, three years for conspiracy to commit kidnapping, 18 years for each of six counts of criminal sexual penetration, 18 months for criminal sexual contact, and 18 months for conspiracy to commit criminal sexual contact.

For his crimes against Cynthia Vigil, Sweazea sentenced Ray to 18 years for kidnapping, nine years for criminal sexual penetration and nine years for conspiracy to commit kidnapping.

Finding Ray's planning and preparation and the horrific nature of his crimes sufficient to constitute aggravation, the judge imposed an additional one third of the total of the forgoing sentences. All sentences, totaling 224 years less two and a half years time served, will be served consecutively.

Ray was remanded to the custody of the New Mexico Department of Corrections.

Jessy Ray goes free

Sentenced to five years of probation

By Bill Johnson of the Desert Journal
Friday, September 21, 2001

Glenda Jean "Jessy" Ray is free with five years of probation ordered for her role in the July 1996 kidnapping of a young woman who her infamous father, David Parker Ray, then raped and sexually tortured for three days.

She had faced 150 years in prison but multiple counts of rape and other charges were dropped.

The prosecution argued that Jessy Ray, 34, delivered to her father, deemed by the FBI to be a criminal sexual sadist, a young woman, Kelly Van Cleave, for his sexual torture pleasure while keeping her unconscious with drugs. All other charges, including several counts of criminal sexual penetration, have been dismissed for Jessy Ray.

It was the videotape of a tattoo on Van Cleave's leg that would lead police to the victim, then living in Colorado, in the wake of the spring 1999 investigation of the Rays and company, all who now hang their heads with serious felony convictions including murder for Dennis Roy Yancy, and the seizure of more than a thousand pieces of evidence from David Ray's home on Bass Road in Elephant Butte Lake State Park, where Ray also worked as a mechanic.

Many friends of Jessy Ray said they thought she would get off easy because she had reported her father's activities to the FBI at least 13 years prior to the 1999 investigation. And some have viewed her as being a victim herself although the truth has yet to be confirmed.

"Jessy Ray actually reported to the FBI her father's activities in 1986. The case of the alleged sexual abuse and slavery of young women and girls was investigated by the FBI in 1986 and 1987 and closed because of insufficient evidence," said Deputy District Attorney Jim Yontz, prosecutor on the trail of torture case for nearly the last two and a half years, "and because they found no victim."

But no one can explain how David Ray's boss, Billy Ray Bowers, at Canal Motors in Phoenix, AZ, disappeared in September 1988. His body rose to the surface at Elephant Butte Lake exactly a year later in

September 1989 and for nine and a half years he would be known as "John Doe." Bowers' body was wrapped in blue tarp, and weighed down by a boat anchor.

The body apparently gassed up during the summer's warm water season at the lake and emerged to the surface when a fisherman found the rolled tarp floating in the Kettle Top area on the east side of the lake. The investigation then revealed that Bowers had been executed and shot in the back of the head before being dumped in the lake.

His identity was unknown until it came up during the investigation of the Ray sexual torture case, Yontz said.

Yontz said Ray traveled between Phoenix and Elephant Butte Lake where he had leased the lot since 1982 or 1984.

But that case apparently will slip through the state's prosecutorial process because, according to Yontz, New Mexico's statute of limitation for murder was 15 years until some three or four years ago when it was extended to the life of the case (or until all suspects are dead).

"We turned this (Bowers' homicide) case over to the U.S. Attorney. It could become a case of the State of Arizona or of the Feds," Yontz said.

While her father spends his life plus in prison, Jessy Ray goes free as her father had wished when he decided to plea out the remaining charges resulting from the kidnappings and rapes of now-deceased Angie Montano of Truth or Consequences in February 1999 and a former Albuquerque prostitute, Cynthia Vigil, in March 1999.

Vigil brought the case to light after she escaped bondage at Ray's residence on Bass Road. Vigil struggled with David Ray's accomplice, Cindy Hendy, broke free and ran outside wearing nothing but a black collar with chain and lock attached.

Ray was found guilty on all counts of kidnapping and criminal sexual penetration in a trial in Estancia earlier in the year for the case involving victim Kelly Van Cleave.

Yontz said a status conference for Jessy Ray on Monday in Socorro turned out instead to be a plea hearing in which she pled no contest to the charge of second degree kidnapping.

District Judge Kevin Sweazea then imposed a nine-year prison sentence, suspended six years and seven months of the sentence and gave Jessy Ray credit of two years and five months for time already served behind bars.

As such, the nine-year sentence is deemed served unless Jessy Ray violates the terms and conditions of her probation, the first year to be under supervised conditions, Yontz said.

If Jessy Ray satisfactorily complies with the terms and conditions of her first year of supervised probation, the Adult Probation and Parole Department can request her remaining time be spent on unsupervised probation, Yontz said.

Asked if Jessy Ray's freedom was a condition for her father to plea guilty to the charges leveled against him, Yontz said, "We told David Ray we were making her this offer. His request and our decision weren't contingent on each other. It was made clear to him we would make the offer to Jessy Ray and it wouldn't void his plea. She was released and is living in Albuquerque," Yontz said.

However, several residents on Austin Avenue in Truth or Consequences reported seeing Jessy Ray in the area during the week or after her release Monday. She was in town to attend her father's sentencing hearing Thursday afternoon.

Yontz said he believes he would have gotten some kind of conviction had the case for Jessy Ray gone to trial. "I believe we could have gotten her convicted for kidnapping but not as an accomplice to rape (in the Van Cleave case only)," Yontz said.

He said the timing of the terrorist attacks back East also affected his case. Much of the evidence in the case was found by FBI agents who are now not available to testify because most all of them have been assigned to investigate the terrorist bombing attacks in the United States, Yontz said.

In a related case, Yontz said kidnap and rape accomplice Cindy Hendy on Wednesday dismissed her appeal on her conviction following her guilty plea in the cases involving Vigil and Montano.

Yontz said Hendy had claimed she received ineffective legal counsel with Las Cruces attorney Xavier Acosta but during Wednesday's hearing in Socorro Hendy withdrew that claim, Yontz said.

Thursday's sentencing for Ray brings closure to the two-and-a-half-year-old case, said Yontz with a sigh of relief.

T or C as seen on the Internet

By Fred Mramor of the Desert Journal
Friday, February 1, 2002

They say there's no such thing as bad publicity as long as they spell your name right. Let's hope this is true because our, shall we say quaint, little town of Truth or Consequences is getting plenty of publicity on the Internet.

In a Google search alone, thousands of websites can be found that refer to T or C in thousands of different ways.

Many of these are innocuous enough, listing T or C's hotels and motels or describing its geography, topography and climate. Nothing wrong with these and they may help attract visitors.

But many other sites display information, or misinformation, which probably isn't what our Chamber of Commerce or Tourism Board would put on the net.

Laurie Kilmartin, a comedian who has appeared on Comedy Central's Premium Blend, relates a story about how a hose ripped away from a gas station's tank when she visited T or C last October.

"From my rearview mirror," the comic reports, "the nozzle and hose appeared eager to get the hell out of Truth or Consequences."

You can read more about her adventures at:

www.kilmartin.com/hoaxes/truth.html.

In his 'Through a Rabbit Windshield Darkly,' Jon Adams at www.jonadams.com in 1987 opines that T or C "isn't much of a town."

Maybe Mr. Adams would be more impressed now that we have an ALCO store and a lovely new fountain on Main Street.

Truth or Consequences is described on a New Mexico Travel Time site as "a pretty grotty town" where "the weirdness factor is high." The author adds, "Erika (whoever that is) tells me that it's undergoing some sort of transformation and become tres chic or something."

For the benefit of anyone reading this article on the Internet and searching for a trendy locale, it should be added that certain elements, who may not be able to afford Taos or Santa Fe, have been trying to make T or C tres chic or something for years.

But attracting the beautiful people to T or C could be a hopeless cause when the cyber wags present another—and perhaps more prevailing—image of this would-be haven for the smart set.

T or C is featured on the White Trash Tour (Revised) at

http://paos.colorado.edu/~arbetter/whitetrash.html

and Zuba, the author of Walking Bitch's White Trash Diner serves up her impression of T or C with a helping of erroneous information about how the town got its name.

www.wb.bappy.com/2000_06_11_oldshit.html

"So yesterday was Ralph Edwards birthday," the Walking Bitch says and continues:

"Ralph Edwards was the host of Truth or Consequences the game show.

"Needless to say, he was from a small town in New Mexico that, you guessed it, renamed the town Truth or Consequences, the longest name of a town in the US, in honor of the 'famous' guy that was from there.

"They have a parade every year through the town, because it is 'Ralph Edwards Day.' YEP nutin like white trash . . . lol.

"How do I know all this?. My sister has lived in Truth or Consequences, NM for about 7 years now, and it never ceases to amaze me the amount of inbreeding that takes place down there.

"People still mine for gold down there for crissakes."

In his must-read article "Truth or Consequences" posted on

www.hayoke.com/id23.htm

Kent Black describes T or C as a town of flinty-eyed cowboys and new-age acolytes and a town of lean expectations and incomes.

It gets worse.

Quoting one T or C resident, Black says, "Or it may be as the retired gentleman on the sidewalk remarked, 'You know what the problem with this town is? Too much damn inbreeding! Look at these people. You can see it. Damn fathers, brothers, sisters, daughters, aunts all sleeping together messing up the damn gene pool!' "

Again with the inbreeding. I seriously doubt that T or C is any more incestuous than other towns, maybe it just has a certain web-toed look about it.

While Black senses that T or C has its "dark side," he seems to have expectations of Truth or Consequences' brighter future.

"Still, for the last several years, people like Waldrum, Howe and Kortemeier have been subtly turning the town in other directions," Black said.

Well that's a little vague but I suppose he means T or C could be chic someday after all.

Christopher Reynolds, a Times Travel writer, says on

http://adserver.latimes.com/

that T or C is a strong candidate for recognition as the weirdest town in the West.

T or C's reputed dark and side weirdness may have inspired a hopeful scriptwriter, or maybe she just found the name intriguing.

At www.socalbrand.com/colb/stories/stalkinghorse.txt the author offers her plot for the TV show X Files in which Agents Scully and Mulder are called to Truth or Consequences, New Mexico, to investigate a series of bizarre murders.

The author in her note says she has created a mythical landscape for Truth or Consequences and admits she has abused dates and times. Her disclaimer: "I dunno, I'm having fun."

Speaking of X Files, unidentified flying objects described as three cylindrical objects, light green in color, were sighted at T or C on Aug. 3, 1952, according to a website located at

www.nicap.dabsol.co.uk/520803.htm.

Almost as surreal as reported UFO sightings is a website whose sole content is the words "I left my heart in Truth or Consequences, New Mexico" four times in four combinations of upper and lower case text.

This little oddity can be found at

www.mcfedries.com/ books/cightml/sstrans.htm

and proves there's a lot of useless junk on the Internet.

But after all the T or C bashing we can take pride, I guess, in being listed on an Odd Town Names site by someone with the improbable name of Turnip Smith.

On this site

www.ks.essortment.com/oddtown_names_ rkom.htm

T or C takes its honored place along with Intercourse, PA, Knockemstiff, OH, and Maggie's Nipples, WY.

Ralph Edwards may not be from Truth or Consequences but neither are a few professional wrestlers who have made T or C their fictitious hometowns.

According to wrestling websites, too numerous to list here, grapplers including Cactus Jack (the most frequently named fictitious favorite son), KroKus Caine (called a Cac Jack wannabe on one sight), Gunslinger and Mankind all hail from Truth or Consequences.

I'm surprised they're not from Knockemstiff.

After reviewing these embarrassing reports about T or C on the Internet, I urge that we, the proud citizens of Truth or Consequences, New Mexico, do all we can to improve its worldwide image.

But right now I gotta get me to the Circle K for an RC Cola and a Moon Pie then meet my cousin Junie Mae under the stands at the tractor pull for a little slap and tickle, 'lessen my uncle gets there first. Ciao.

David Ray dies after three years served of his 224-year prison term

"Satan has a place for you, I hope you burn in hell forever," said Berta Vigil, grandmother of one of Ray's sexual torture victims.

Desert Journal Staff Report
May 31, 2002

Rape and kidnapping victim Cynthia Vigil's grandmother's wish may come true. Unless, of course, David Ray really repented and came clean with God.

David Parker Ray, sentenced to 224 years in prison last September after his conviction on numerous offenses involving the abduction and sexual torture of three young women at his Elephant Butte Lake home, died Tuesday night, May 28, at the prison in Hobbs, NM.

Ray, 62, had been credited with two and a half years of jail time served since his sentencing to prison eight months ago.

Ray and his accomplice, Cindy Hendy, were arrested in March 1999 after his very last victim, Cynthia Vigil, escaped his home donned in only a collar and chain.

A Torrance County jury convicted Ray for his crimes against Kelly Van Cleave, formerly of Truth or Consequences, in 1996. He later pled guilty to charges involving two other victims, the late Angie Montano of T or C and Cynthia Vigil of Albuquerque, in 1999.

FBI agent Mary Ellen O'Toole had testified at Ray's sentencing hearing that examination of Ray's home, the trailer he had converted into his infamous "toy box" and the sexual paraphernalia and drawings found there suggested that Ray was a "criminal sexual sadist."

Ray's toy box and custom equipment were extremely impressive in terms of sexual sadism, potential lethality and the time, money and effort it took to keep them a secret, the FBI said.

Ray's victims and the victims' family members had made their wishes known to the court and to Ray before the judge pronounced sentence last September.

Kelly (Van Cleave) Garrett said she wanted Ray to live a for a long time and suffer in prison where she hoped he would be controlled and used in the same manner that she and Ray's other victims had.

Loretta Romero, Angie Montano's mother, said her daughter had a good heart but had lost all respect, lost her smile, lost everything because of David Ray. Mrs. Romero said she was here for Angie (who had died from pneumonia after her case came to light) and her two little boys whose lives Ray had ruined.

Mrs. Romero said she felt sorry for David Ray, that she forgives him and that her daughter would forgive him. But Angie's mother said she will never forget.

Less forgiving was Cynthia Vigil's grandmother, Bertha Vigil. Mrs. Vigil told Ray he was a poor excuse for a human being and asked him how he would like for her to do to his daughter what he had done to Cynthia.

Bertha Vigil said her granddaughter has nightmares every night and that Ray had ruined not only her life but those of her whole family. Cynthia's grandmother said she prays Ray will suffer every day for the rest of his life.

"Satan has a place for you. I hope you burn in hell forever," Mrs. Vigil said.

"I bare scars outside and inside that will never heal," Cynthia Vigil said. She said no punishment is equal to the agony she has suffered.

Vigil said she is afraid of being tied down and helpless, of the dark and of going out alone. Cynthia Vigil, crying, said she hoped David Ray would spend the rest of his life between four walls and suffer the way he made her suffer.

"This monster should never be allowed to walk the streets again," said prosecuting attorney Jim Yontz during Ray's sentencing. "There should be no light at the end of the tunnel and he should realize that a cell will be his home for the rest of his life and that he will leave only in a box."

Ray reportedly died in his cell at 8:30 p.m. Tuesday. Prison officials said they didn't immediately know his cause of death but suspected it was from a known heart condition that he often complained about while in custody and received treatment for on taxpayers' account.

He is survived by his daughter, Glenda Jean "Jessy" Ray, who was sentenced last year to five years on probation for her role in the 1996 rape case.

Ray had told the court that no one but his attorney had heard his side. Ray said many lies and distortions were told in his case.

Ray said he had entered into a plea agreement to effect his daughter's release. Jessy Ray was Ray's accomplice in the abduction and sexual torture of Kelly Van Cleave.

Ray had said the two and a half years in confinement since his arrest had allowed him to reflect, read his Bible and "get right with God." Ray said he has put his life in His hands and that he can't change the past but can only be sorry.

<<< >>>

State police divers return empty handed late Tuesday afternoon after a two-day extensive underwater search at Elephant Butte Lake for bodies that may have been dumped by David Ray during his reign of sexual terror at the lake. Click on photo for more shots & story.

DJ Photo by Bill Johnson

Agents seek closure on David Ray's case

No bodies found in EB Lake after two-day intensive search

By Bill Johnson of the Desert Journal
Friday, November 22, 2002

After two days of intensive searching for bodies believed to have been dumped in Elephant Butte Lake during deceased convict David Parker Ray's reign of sexual torture, more than a dozen state police divers returned home empty handed late Tuesday afternoon.

Murky and cold are the words divers chose to describe conditions during their search for possible homicide victims whose most likely remains would consist of bones considering the fact that it has been more than three and a half years

...Cold & murky

These were the words state police divers (top photo) used to describe their search Monday and Tuesday at Elephant Butte Lake for any bones or remnants that could be tied to the David Ray sexual torture case. They dove primarily in the Kettle Top area (middle photo) that is among the deepest areas of the reservoir. The dock at Rock Canyon Marina (bottom photo) is where state police and park rangers floated in the body of Billy Ray Bowers in 1989—his body wrapped in blue tarp and weighed down with a boat anchor. Bowers was Ray's boss at Canal Motors in Phoenix, AZ, at the time.

DJ photos by Bill Johnson

since Ray's arrest in March 1999 on charges of multiple kidnappings and rapes in which he held his victims captive while sexually torturing them for days on end.

But no homicides thus far have been tied to Ray although his former boss Billy Ray Bowers at Canal Motors in Phoenix, AZ, rose to the surface of the lake in 1989.

And it was in the Kettle Top area of the east side of the lake where Bowers' body emerged while wrapped in blue tarp with a boat anchor attached.

Investigators then knew him only as the anonymously slain "John Doe" and had determined that he had been executed—shot in the back of the head—before being disposed of in the lake a year prior in 1988. It would take nearly a year for his body to gas up enough to cause the weight of the tarp, body and anchor to rise from its reservoir gravesite.

And then it took another 10 years or the week after David Ray was arrested before they actually knew Bowers' identity.

The location of Bower's body when it was found, combined with witnesses' statements and evidence collected from Ray's "Toy Box"—the sound-proofed travel trailer chambers in which he held his young female victims captive and tortured for days at a time—also led Criminal Agent Norman Rhoades and the team of 14 New Mexico State Police divers to the Kettle Top area to conduct their search earlier this week.

Rhoades said Ray kept pictures and illustrations of Kettle Top—a mesa shaped like a kettle—including one that ran in the Desert Journal.

And Ray was no stranger to the lake, having worked as a mechanic in the Elephant Butte Lake State Park's shop for several years. Being a boating enthusiast, he often took his daughter, Jessy Ray, and her female friends on boating excursions on Elephant Butte Lake.

One of his daughter's friends, Becky, who says she was lucky to never have been one of Ray's victims possibly because she affectionately called him "Dad," went on these boating trips with the Rays.

She recalled friendly conversations she had with David Ray while on the lake. Like the time she asked, "I wonder if there are any bodies in there," and Ray would respond, "Lots of them." Or how Ray would comment as they passed over certain spots, "These are the deepest parts."

And no doubt the Kettle Top area is among the deepest parts of the lake, possibly second only to the depths of Elephant Butte Dam.

And Kettle Top would be the preferred place to dump bodies because it's a lot more remote—thus easier to escape detection—than the dam area where a marina, restaurant and bar, cabins and residences are situated.

But, one statement Ray made on a boating trip in particular came to Becky's mind after Ray's arrest. She recalled telling him about boyfriend troubles she was having at the time and Ray explained what to do in such a case:

"After killing him, you cut him open, fill up his body with rocks and wrap it with chicken wire (to hold the rocks in place), then dump him in the lake."

...Are bodies buried in the lake?

There have been in the past—Billy Ray Bowers of Phoenix and Janice Pulliam of Albuquerque whose homicides are still unsolved since their bodies were discovered in Elephant Butte Lake in the late 1980s. The question should be, will any more be found? Any new finds will be tagged to David Ray and then ruled out, investigators said Tuesday after their two-day underwater search. The camera's angle from the dock at South Rock Canyon is a possibility of where divers might look—and they have been looking there—as this area contains lots of depth and remoteness.

DJ Photo by Bill Johnson

And there was also the time when David Ray told his latest flame and accomplice Cindy Hendy—now serving 35 years in prison for her role in the kidnaps and rapes of two women in February and March 1999—that he had put 18 bodies to rest in the lake, according to investigators.

So, put together, one would expect other bodies besides Bowers' would be discovered by now except Ray learned the first time after Bowers' body gassed up and rose to the surface: "you cut 'em up and fill 'em up with rocks."

But Rhoades and the diving crew found no such thing laying on the bottom of the reservoir although Rhoades admits it's like looking for a needle in a haystack.

"We covered the area that recedes back toward Kettle Top where it's only 40 feet down now. The last time we searched a couple of years ago it was at a depth of 90 feet to 110 feet," Rhoades said.

The difference in depths is the result of the severe ongoing drought. And in spite of poor or zero visibility at the bottom of the lake (and most of the lake), divers still managed to cover a large area south and west of Kettle Top, Rhoades said. He said the divers ran lines along the bottom of the lake and if a line snagged on something they would check it out.

The landscape around Rock Canyon Marina has changed greatly with prolonged drought and lower lake elevations but this is generally the area where ambulance crews recovered the body of Billy Ray Bowers about 14 years ago.

DJ photo by Bill Johnson

"Nothing was found. There is still a lot of area not covered," he said.

The reason for the search and other current activities in this case is to bring closure to it, Rhoades said. "We hope to close out this case by March," he added.

Even if closed, if something pops up in the future the case would be restored to active status.

And any bodies or body parts that may be found at the lake well into the future will be tied to the Ray case whether or not he did it and although Ray died May 28 in prison in Hobbs from a heart attack while serving out his 224-year term.

To aid in the identification of any possible victims, state police released photos of jewelry and clothing items, including a couple of purses, that were among the 2,000 pieces of evidence that they and agents of the Federal Bureau of Investigation seized from Ray's lease lot property on Bass Road in the Hot Springs Landing area of Elephant Butte Lake State Park.

The photographs of these items are being displayed for possible identification of their owners on Albuquerque's Channel 13 News website at krqe.com.

Rhoades said the KRQE website's special project for David Ray received more than 130,000 hits since it was posted last week. He said that as a result of the project, he has one lead to follow up on when he returns to his command post.

State police, state park rangers and Sierra County sheriff's deputies wait at the edge of Elephant Butte Lake where the body of Billy Ray Bowers of Phoenix, AZ, still wrapped in blue tarp, is found in late September 1989. Bowers was David Ray's supervisor at Canal Motors in Phoenix at the time.

DJ photo by Bill Johnson

The Shadow Advisory

By Bill Johnson of the Desert Journal
Friday, February 14, 2003

...Second David Ray book is more fiction than fact

One thing disgusts me more than anything else in my profession—wanton disregard for the truth. I suppose that's why I'm in this business—a poor one indeed—and why crime authors like Jim Fielder of Seattle, WA, can soak up the bucks writing trash—pure trash, even knowing the truth.

I wouldn't be writing what I'm about to convey if not for the fact that one particular section of Fielder's book, *Slow Death*—a second book about David Parker Ray and his infamous sexual torture case at Elephant Butte Lake released last month and only a half year after English author John Glatt's book *Cries in the Desert* was released in June 2002—is absolutely false and only a few people know it, including Fielder. That's because I told him the truth, but he chose to ignore it and chose to listen to only one side of the story.

Since I was a witness, I know what I'm talking about. I was there and everything I am about to say is the truth—no dispute about it.

In talking about Dennis Roy Yancy—now serving a 20-year prison term for the murder of young mother Marie Parker—and his youthful years dabbling in Satanism, Fielder wrote (last paragraph, page 80):

"The Sentinel went so far as to hire an undercover reporter to infiltrate the [occult-related] gang and report on their evil ways."

Wrong—the *Sentinel* publishers never knew about the Satanic gang until the Sentinel's photojournalist, who was NOT hired to be undercover anything, told them about it just before Halloween 1987.

This particular *Sentinel* employee, whose name I shall keep anonymous as he wishes me to do (he'll only talk to police), was hired to do routine everyday newspaper work, and I think I also remember that he may have worked as a disc jockey at KCHS Radio

Station, which also belongs to the *Sentinel* publishers. I know, I worked alongside him day after day and he is among the best of my friends to this day. And I told Fielder about it during one of his few phone calls to my office since the David Ray case broke in March 1999.

Sentence two, same paragraph: "The reporter got sucked into the group and refused to expose his new friends."

Wrong again, very, very wrong. My friend, the photojournalist, never knew the gang members or Yancy personally.

What my friend did do, however, was attach himself to Sierra County's multi-agency task force that was formed to investigate occult related crimes, including the activities of Yancy and his friends.

My friend the photojournalist became very involved (perhaps over-involved) with this task force, which consisted of city police, sheriff's office, state police and even included retired District Attorney's Office Investigator John Ashbaugh (I think he was working as an investigator for the sheriff's office at that time 15 years ago.)

Third sentence, same paragraph: "One of those friends was Dennis [Roy] Yancy."

Other witnesses to my friend's involvement will testify, I mean swear on the Bible, that my friend the photojournalist never befriended Yancy or never infiltrated Yancy's gang like a spy. What a joke. These witnesses include Mike Worley and Ricky McNutt, both former employees of KCHS. They too will know the truth, all of it, just like author Fielder did because I told him about it. But he did not yield to the truth.

Fourth sentence, same paragraph: "The reporter was fired by the Sentinel, but not before five-year-old Frances Baird's grandfather (Neil R. Baird, died 1992) wrote a blistering editorial condemning the activities of Dennis Roy Yancy and his ilk."

Another lie and that could have only come from the unknowing—I was there more than Neil's widow, Myrna Baird Kohs, or than little Frances because I got stuck in the middle of a dispute between Neil Baird and my friend the photojournalist.

My friend the photojournalist was NOT fired—he quit. Why? Because Neil violated my friend's trust. My friend the photojournalist divulged information about the task force and its activities to Baird in confidence. Nothing was supposed to be leaked or released about the occult related gang until after the multi-agency task force completed its investigation.

My friend made an agreement with police that nothing would get published until after police finished their probe. Seems reasonable enough—like every other investigation, give the police time and eventually you'll get a good story and not disrupt or interfere with the probe.

At the time, I was caught between a rock and a hard place. On one hand, I agreed with my friend the photojournalist that confidence should be kept by the editor but Neil Baird chose to publish some information before the multi-agency task force completed their probe, thus disrupting its progress and virtually ending it.

On the other hand, at the time I didn't clearly understand the agreement my friend had made with police to withhold possible public information. In other words, I thought he was keeping the public in the dark and uninformed at the time. I tried to persuade him that what Baird did, even though prematurely, may have been in the public's interest.

But my friend was so angry with Baird that he quit, even after I begged and pleaded for him to stay on the *Sentinel* team. But now I understand my friend's reasons for quitting and the need to keep confidentiality between reporters and editors and not disrupt a police investigation by leaking sensitive information in published reports.

Now that I think about, Neil stole all of the glory from my friend the photojournalist by writing his shallow editorial (which I won't repeat here).

If Baird had waited, my friend the photojournalist would have developed a very comprehensive report (perhaps a prize winner) with numerous photographs to prove the occult activities that were going on in Sierra County at the time (and they still are, to some degree). And the people of Sierra County would have been better informed about the occult-related crimes and activities that were taking place around them.

But that would never happen because my friend QUIT and all the public got was Baird's sputtering, meaningless words.

Make no mistake about it, Mr. Fielder, you knew that too because this was another fact I told you that you chose to ignore in your incredulous book. What a shame and a waste of good paper.

Because a whole paragraph is riddled with lies and deceit, I only wonder how much more of Fielder's book misleads readers. The publishers should have called it a fictional piece and given David Ray and his cohorts different identities.

I have heard several other complaints from other readers of Fielder's book and I also want to expose other lies—like the $12 million jet that the Full Gospel Tabernacle purportedly owns. Hell, they can't even keep their bus running!

Or how a "murder" suspect killed Sheriff's Deputy Kelly Clark when the suspect was involved in grand theft with no previous homicides haunting his criminal history.

Or how then-sheriff Terry Byers could be blamed for Deputy

Clark's death when her transport was of a prisoner who wasn't considered dangerous and who probably was going to be released in three months anyway. Perhaps the blame should be put on the murderer and the lack of communication from jail staff for not telling the transporting officer about the prisoner's violent tendencies, such as throwing food through his cell's bars earlier that day or week. Clark's death was not Byers' fault, no sir, yet petty stupid people and even Fielder's book still blame him to this day.

And I must question smutty crime author Fielder's motives for glorifying the *Sentinel* and Frances Baird (but I'm sure she deserves maybe some pittance of recognition for being a young cub reporter on the beat) when it was the *Desert Journal* that won nearly all of the press awards for its David Ray coverage. Where are the Sentinel's honors? There are none! What a sham! I'm sure Fielder got what he paid for—a bunch of trash.

I would recommend to readers John Glatt's *Cries in the Desert* although I know it also contains some inaccuracies. Yet Glatt's book seems to exclude the flat-out lies, disregard for the truth and to hell with the readers' right to know the truth that are ever so prevalent in Fielder's *Slow Death.*

I hope *Slow Death* takes a fast death and doesn't reprint any second or additional editions unless the publishers care to iron out the truth and stick it in too.

The Shadow Advisory

By Bill Johnson of the Desert Journal
Friday, February 28, 2003

**...Orgytown, USA:
Do you know where
your kids are tonight?**

Slow Death by Jim Fielder, Page 168—"On Nov. 12, 1999, the Desert Journal ran an interview with Jeannie Astbury in which she claimed that Roy Yancy raped her at David Ray's mobile home. The masthead for the Desert Journal read IN HOT PURSUIT OF THE TRUTH, but Jim Yontz always called it the 'Deserted Journal' because it had the smallest number of readers of the three weeklies in T or C."

The book goes on to quote the interview of Astbury as published by the Desert Journal nearly four years ago.

P. 171—In a conversation between Deputy District Attorney Jim Yontz and Sierra County Sentinel cub reporter Francis Baird, Fielder wrote, quoting Yontz again:

"In the state of New Mexico, you can't prosecute someone without a body—and without any evidence. We don't have anything other than Dennis (Roy Yancy) admitting to us that he did the dirty deed [kill Marie Parker in July 1997]."

"What about the article in the [Desert] Journal about Jeannie Astbury?" asked [Francis] Baird.

"No way," said Yontz. "I couldn't use her because the 'Deserted' Journal had her memory hypnotically refreshed. Juries don't like that kind of testimony."

It seems the author of *Slow Death* used our material without permission—I never gave Jim Fielder my nod, verbal or written, to take direct quotes out of the Desert Journal. I suppose we're even now because his publisher didn't give me permission to quote my own stuff out of their book, for which I'm not fairly compensated, oh well…

As was the case two weeks ago when I wrote my raving review that demonstrated and proved how four sentences in a single paragraph of Fielder's book were pure hype with no truth, I since finished reading the entire book and found more falsehoods and deceptions, apparently all in the name of making Francis Baird look like the queen bee of reporters, maybe so she could go work alongside Jim Fielder at the Seattle rag.

Don't get me wrong, I respect Francis and think she's got a million times more smarts than her grandmother. At age 11 she was resolving publisher-editor related disputes in the newspaper office where she had grown up since the day she was born. And her asking Yontz about a Desert Journal article shows she still respected us, or else she would never have considered using us as her source for that particular quote in the book.

First off, Yontz is from Socorro and the only way he would think that we were the 'Deserted' Journal rather than the Desert Journal is if Francis or her grandmother or anyone at the Sentinel told him the same lie they've been telling everyone else, including all of our advertisers, thus clouding and prejudicing Yontz's view.

I have caught their advertising sale representatives in the middle of this lie through phone calls made by my staff and they claimed we had a circulation of only 400—I'm sure that's what they're still saying over there at brand X.

But at the time the David Ray sexual trail of torture story broke (of which the Desert Journal was among the first, if not the first, to report) and the months afterward, our circulation soared from 900 to more than 1,200 copies sold each week.

That may not seem like much to many, but for a recently established newspaper it was quite an unexpected growth.

The Desert Journal had a readership of 3.84 readers per copy, according to our March 1999 survey of 50 paid subscribers. With 1,232 copies sold weekly in 1999, that would mean our readership was 4,731 weekly—about half of Sierra County's population then.

Our printer says the Los Angeles Times would be jealous over a market that took in 50 percent of the readers, never mind 50 percent of the entire population (not everyone is a reader)—that 25% of the share of the market is quite decent itself.

So, eat your words, Jim Yontz!

Let's discuss Yontz's workplace, the District Attorney's office with whom the Desert Journal lost all of its respect and confidence while Ron Lopez was the elected DA. For those of our readers who remember, it was the DA's office that screwed up the prosecution of the two suspects involved in the drive-by shooting of our office when we were still on Austin Avenue in October 1998.

The DA's office intentionally lost evidence during the preliminary hearing for a local doctor, who police accused of doing the shooting. The investigator of the DA's office at the time, John Ashbaugh, said after the two suspects' arrests that the DA's office had a solid case against both suspects, especially the doctor.

Then we watched the case fall apart in court, and on the stand the defense tried to make me—the victim—look like the villain, all without any objection from the DA's office prosecutor.

So, you see, relations suddenly became strained and we made damned sure Ron Lopez would never be elected the DA again. Thank God the voters had enough sense to get him out of office.

Ron Lopez had hired Yontz to cover the David Ray et al case and so I'm sure Yontz heard a lot of prejudicial stuff against us—not from only the DA's office but especially from the Sentinel people.

Yontz saying that we're the "Deserted" Journal is a slap in the face to all small businesses who want to have a piece of the American pie, who dream that someday they'll be big. He's the type who never cheers for the underdog—he has to make the sure bet that he'll be the winner. No risk there, is there? I call that cowardice. I always sing my loudest for the little guy because that's where freedom starts and imperialism croaks.

Let's talk about who the "shrimpy" ("deserted" in Yontz's own word as quoted by Fielder) guys are now.

Well the "Deserted" Journal has grown tremendously the last year with the addition of its online version, www.desertjournalonline.com, and combined with the Desert Journal newspaper, both now kick the Sentinel's and Herald's butts in terms of readership. So, Mr. Yontz, you can sob in despair on your deserted corner of the gutter.

Author Jim Fielder also lies about the Jeannie Astbury interview and makes it look like we interfered in the investigation of the David Ray case.

First of all, Ms. Astbury never said she was raped by Yancy in Ray's mobile home—she frankly never knew where it happened. And yes, the Desert Journal hired a local naturopath healer to do interviews of two women who couldn't remember the events of their times with the David Ray gang, specifically Ray's daughter Jessy Ray and their friend Dennis Roy Yancy, because both women had been drugged and they wanted to know if something happened to them while they were unconscious or semi-conscious.

So they were put under hypnosis (actually just a relaxation technique). Jeannie's memory of the events became clearer but the other woman was still cloudy about the events in her dealings with Jessy Ray.

No memories were refreshed, as Yontz purports, because no suggestions were made to either woman. The women refreshed their own memories through relaxation and nothing else.

At no time did we ever discuss their ability to become witnesses or new victims in the David Ray et al case although Jeannie did talk to an investigator on a few occasions. We never even considered it.

The state and Yontz never would have known about Jeannie or her rape allegations against Yancy if it hadn't been for our efforts at the Desert Journal.

Fielder's book is vile and disgusting and paints Truth or Consequences, NM, as Orgytown, USA, where orgies and meth making are common place, no, I mean "rampant" among "all" of the people here.

He quotes Sierra County Sentinel Publisher Myrna Baird as saying through her granddaughter Francis that when she (Myrna Baird) and her husband Neil moved to Truth or Consequences [in the mid 1960s to buy KCHS radio station with money Neil's half-brother loaned him] she was told by locals that if they didn't swap wives they would be out of business in no time.

I'm sure this was true for Myrna. And look—she's still in business today! And when I worked there at her barn for 11 years she said the same thing about police officers swapping their wives, which I never knew to be true, but maybe she knew something I didn't.

But no one ever approached me, or my wife, and said or suggested the same about swapping wives to stay in business when we decided to establish the Desert Journal. At our open house celebrating our debut, good, honest people including then-Mayor Lois Reaver-Black, Bud and Betty Whitmore, and many others came. Never once was sex on the agenda but Fielder would have the world think that we in T or C are a bunch of perverts who cook up meth in our kitchens all day and screw each other in mass to no end.

Maybe that's because Fielder listened to nothing but a bunch of pathological liars and then quoted them in his dirty, filthy book. What a sorry day for the townspeople of T or C to allow these bastards to reign over the town like they're all our little gods.

In the book, Fielder quotes locals as saying the Full Gospel Tabernacle is the devil's church, without justification or without backing up what he says. My wife's son would really appreciate being called a devil worshipper when he never touched an illegal substance in his life and never engaged in any abnormal behavior, which according to Fielder, runs amuck in our city in orgy style, in the hot bath establishments on Austin Avenue.

I remember when Fielder told me on the phone in a factual tone of voice after the outbreak of the sexual torture case four years ago that everyone must be sexually deviant in T or C. I told him that's a piss poor label to give to a town with mostly retirees and churchgoers.

Of course this town has its share of sexually perverted criminals, but every town in America has them, and I'm sure Seattle, Fielder's hometown, has its share too. I'm beginning to think that with all of the vulgarity he wrote in his book he may be on the looming edge of becoming one himself.

Slow Death can burn in hell at Fahrenheit 351 along with David Ray and his likes.

The Shadow Advisory

By Bill Johnson of the Desert Journal
Friday, March 7, 2003

...Sierra County has lots more to offer than the stigma attached to David Ray

Some people have been telling me that Truth or Consequences is in a state of decay, that the trend may be irreversible, all because of the national attention that highlights the notorious Trail of Sexual Torture case brought on by David Parker Ray and his gang of sick sexual predators.

I say these people are probably on their way out of town—perhaps their vacancies will be filled by those who give a damn and who want to make a difference.

I keep hearing that business is doomed to fail but I personally wouldn't stay in business if I didn't think there was at least a minuscule chance for financial success. We already proved professional success with the showering of some 30 New Mexico Press Association awards for excellence in newspaper and website work the last six years of our seven years plus existence.

But the Desert Journal isn't the only thing that is making the grade in Sierra County. You can't count all of the great things, never mind all of the great people, that inhabit our community on the fingers and toes of both hands and feet.

Pretty soon, memories of sexual sadist David Parker Ray and his infamous toy box, the torture chamber where he played with many of his kidnapped victims, will fade away as they have of other notorious criminals like America's Most Wanted Ed Maurice Barbara of the 1980s era mining scam fame.

This furniture salesman of the San Francisco Bay area came to Sierra County to try his luck at digging up gold. Rather than digging, he painted gold and sold securities in his bogus gold mine while flaunting an aura of legitimacy, engaging the then-sheriff and a security guard in a bribery scheme.

You hardly ever hear talk about Barbara anymore unless you're a prospector who thinks that rather than dying of cancer in Florida under an alias and then getting cremated (all according to his wife) he instead took his millions of dollars in loot to Barbados to enjoy the rest of his life (while his poor elderly victims starve).

David Ray won't have that luxury. Instead of fleeing justice, he got caught, convicted and permanently locked up and recently died from a heart condition. It won't be long before people say, "David who?"

In the meantime, let's look at our community's and its people's accomplishments and honors, starting with our retirees who always seem to rise and shine while the rest of us sleep: for examples, Norman Allish, 87, multiple gold medallist National Senior Olympics swimmer; and Lee Belle Johnson, (she's gotta be getting close to 90), cowgirl poet who recites myriads of her poems from memory and who has been nominated to the National Cowgirl Hall of Fame.

Then there are also the youth of the community—our pride and joy—who excel in their endeavors to make their world a better place, whether it's being named to all-state band or all-state chorus, participating in the Army JROTC, etc. We have hundreds of examples of exemplary youth who make a difference and who make the grade.

I see hope where nay-sayers see no light at the end of the tunnel. It's up to all of us to make a difference if we want to see positive change.

But there will always be those who want to drag the community down. They do the dirty deeds by manufacturing and trafficking methamphetamine, by murdering or raping the innocent, by whatever destructive means possible.

It's time we change our image for the better, strive to achieve some sense of community pride, or else get the hell out of Dodge.

The Shadow Advisory

By Bill Johnson of the Desert Journal
Friday, March 14, 2003

...Safe Community?

If you were to ask me whether I thought Truth or Consequences is a safe community, I wouldn't even blink. "Hell, no!" I'd have to tell you.

But if you were me, you'd understand why I would say that, right? If you don't, you don't know me. And if you don't believe me, then you're a liar, at least to yourself because what I have to say is the truth.

Justice is blind in Truth or Consequences. A lot of people suffer because she is a pig-headed blinded bitch. Its name itself is cursed.

But I love this community and I will make a difference! Tough love is here. Mark my words!

Christ told his disciples he would sing to the rocks because at least the rocks had ears. The rocks could listen. Maybe that's why I took up rock hounding as a hobby. The rocks would listen to me. Finally, something would hear my voice. A lonely voice in the desert, singing to the rocks...

Let's talk about my voice for just a second—I'm not the easiest person to listen to and, as a matter of fact, I like to do all of my business in writing. My hands control what I have to say in writing. My mouth does not.

And if I were to do as Apostle Paul instructed a troubled church with members ("body parts" in his words) gone astray, and the actual need to sever their relationship from the body, I'd be cutting off my tongue.

Truth is like a clashing cymbal. So back to my topic, the safety of the community—how safe is it?

Well, some people never get their justice, while the criminals do. They get to take home the bread and butter; the victims get screwed.

If you don't know what I mean, come pay a visit to my office or set up an appointment with me. And if I trust you, I'll tell you the truth. If I don't trust you, I'll say nothing.

But if those who would harm me get in my way, they'll have to face one god-awful army of vengeance. Whether I stand alone, separated from the rest of the world which has gone all to hell, I still will have my say.

And if the community isn't listening, perhaps the rocks will.

If you read this message, send me a postcard, e-mail, a note through the door, a message on the phone—just something to let me know that I haven't died and gone to hell where it appears that the people are more deaf than me, who is half deaf, or a lot more than half deaf, but who still tries to listen and even YELLS to try to get an answer.

Send to me at Desert Journal, P.O. Box 215., Truth or Consequences, NM 87901; phone 505-894-7341; e-mail at_desertjournal@zianet.com.

Let me know how you feel about the safety of our community, whether it be Truth or Consequences, Sierra County, and/or New Mexico. If I deem your comment publish worthy, I'll run it in the letters to the editor. If it's great, I might even break it out and make it a guest editorial.

But is the community safe? You tell me!

I already told you how I feel. And if you didn't catch it the first time, stick around, maybe you'll hear it again, that is if you care to listen to a loud guy like me.

Notice I didn't say "soft spoken" because I'm not. But that's only because I know no one is listening and maybe the rocks are. Right? Tell me about that too!

Agent Norman Rhoades

T or C's first child porn possession case unfolds [1]

A few books and other explicit materials involving mostly young boys gets gay man into trouble

By Bill Johnson of the Desert Journal
Friday, March 21, 2003

Agent Norman Rhoades of the New Mexico State Police Criminal Investigation Section has cracked Sierra County's first child pornography possession case.

Rhoades leveled a criminal complaint against a professed homosexual whose "closet" in Truth or Consequences got exposed in court Thursday.

The storage unit that the gay man rented in Truth or Consequences allegedly contained several books depicting sexual acts between men and boys and other unlawful materials that portray the sexual exploitation of children.

Anthony Rodriquez, 36, of Las Cruces and a former resident of Truth or Consequences, now faces a fourth degree felony charge of sexual exploitation of children.

Agent Rhoades filed the charge against Rodriguez in magistrate court on March 20. According to the criminal complaint, Rodriquez "willfully, deliberately possessed material that contained sexual exploitation of children, contrary to NMSA 1978, Section 30-6A-3."

The charge pails in comparison to the events that led up to Agent Rhoades' arrest of Rodriquez on Monday, including allegations that

---

[1] Editor's Note: This story is being published in this book because of the implications of another serious sexual perversion that got exposed in Truth or Consequences as a result of the investigation in the David Ray case. The people definitely have a right to know to protect their children from child molesters.

Rodriquez's deceased homosexual lover James Bryant had maintained books and videotapes containing child pornography and snuff-films inside his residence and that Bryant delved in sexual fantasies involving babies, playing the role with his lover Rodriquez.

Magistrate Thomas Pestak set bond for Rodriquez at $50,000 cash surety during the defendant's first appearance in court Thursday.

For Rhoades, the case goes all of the way back to April 19, 1999, about a month after the infamous Elephant Butte trail of sexual torture case involving David Parker Ray broke.

Rhoades, an agent of the CIS for 22 years, said he was assigned to the case involving sexual torture, abduction and rape that involved several victims. He said during the course of the David Ray investigation, an activist against child exploitation, D.J. Welch, told him that James Bryant, a resident of Truth or Consequences at the time, was an active member of the North American Man/Boy Love Association (NAMBLA).

Welch also told the agent that Bryant was involved with abduction and sexual penetration and contact of children. Welch further informed Rhoades that two homosexual males reported Bryant maintained the child porno and snuff films inside his East Riverside Drive residence on the east, or rural, side of the Rio Grande by what is also known as the second footbridge.

"This information was related to the Truth or Consequences City Police Department," Agent Rhoades said in the statement of facts in support of the criminal complaint.

Not long after the unrelated David Ray case came to light, Bryant moved to San Miguel, Mexico, near Mexico City.

It wouldn't be until nearly four years later when another egg would crack revealing lots more about Bryant's character. Rhoades said T or C resident James Pendle told him on March 3 this year that Bryant had committed suicide while living in Las Cruces at 1421 Wyoming St.

Las Cruces police detective Greg Garcia told Rhoades that Bryant shot and killed himself inside his home on Feb. 2, now about six weeks ago. The death occurred while Bryant was living with Anthony Rodriquez.

The next day after the Pendle interview, or March 4, Agent Rhoades and Det. Garcia paid a visit to Rodriquez at his home where Rodriquez told them that Bryant indeed had been a member of the NAMBLA organization and that Bryant had tried to recruit him as a member.

Rodriquez said he knew Bryant for about five years and lived with him for a short time in T or C. Rhoades also learned that Bryant had returned from Mexico and relocated to Las Cruces about a year before his death.

"[I] learned from Anthony Rodriquez that he and James Bryant were homosexual partners and enjoyed sexual encounters using leather and chain devices but he (Rodriquez) soon learned that Bryant's sexual preference [was] with young boys and infants," Rhoades said in the statement of facts.

Rodriquez told Rhoades that he and Bryant many times role-played fantasies where they would pretend to engage in sexual intercourse with young boys and male infants, although Rodriquez said he neither engaged in nor actually observed such acts between Bryant and children, according to the agent's statement.

During their sexual encounters, the role playing involved Rodriquez acting the part of the infant or young boy and they both would engage in sexual penetration of a teddy bear while fantasizing it was an infant, according to the agent's statement.

Rodriquez said he and Bryant both had discussed purchasing a toy doll to replace the teddy bear, according to Rhoades' statement.

But that's not all, Rodriquez told the agent that he and Bryant would drive to Burn Lake in Las Cruces and while seated in their vehicle they would masturbate while watching children at play. Also while in other public places, Bryant would ask Rodriquez whether he noticed a certain young boy.

"[I] learned from Rodriquez that he and Bryant planned to adopt a young boy and had no concerns for the child's safety from abuse from Bryant," Agent Rhoades said in his statement of facts.

Rodriquez said he and Bryant approached Rodriquez's sister with a request that she become pregnant from a donor, which would be her brother Rodriquez, and after the child of incest was born, to relinquish the child to the custody of Rodriquez and Bryant.

Rhoades said Rodriquez also reported that he and Bryant traveled to Juarez, Mexico, where Bryant would give a young boy a dollar bill to see if the boy would follow them. Bryant spoke of renting a motel room to engage in sexual acts with the young boy, Rodriquez told Rhoades.

Bryant also spoke of purchasing a farm in Mexico where they could keep young boys for sexual acts after abducting them, Rodriquez said during his interview with Rhoades earlier this month.

Rodriquez said he was still conditioned from his sexual relationship with Bryant and that he still had tendencies toward fantasizing sexual encounters with children "and alluded to what he referred to as his favorite book titled Fathers, which depicts several photographic images of nude men holding nude infants and young children," according to the agent's statement.

Rhoades also learned from Rodriquez that his former pastor, Reverend Felix Gonzalez, destroyed all of the child pornography that Bryant had possessed the day after Bryant died and that none was left in the home.

However, Rodriquez disclosed that Bryant was renting a storage unit at National Self Storage facility in Truth or Consequences but that he didn't know what was inside of it.

Rodriquez eventually told the agent that he did have some items inside his home that belonged to Bryant that "may contain child pornography and subsequently relinquished those items to the two lawmen, Rhoades and Garcia.

The items allegedly belonging to Bryant included: photographic images of nude young boys; printed stories and books containing stories of incidents of sexual acts with young boys; documentation relating to Diaper Pail Friends, an organization where adults role play being an infant to include wearing diapers and acting like an infant; several books and documentation relating to the NAMBLA organization that condones sexual interaction between adults and children; a catalog of items related to Diaper Pail Friends; correspondence from Diaper Pail Friends which indicated that Bryant had joined the organization, and a CD-R disc that Rodriquez said contained stories of sexual acts involving children, according to Rhoades' statement.

On March 5, National Self Storage employee Karen Donaldson told Agent Rhoades and Det. Garcia during their visit to the T or C storage unit facility that not only Bryant, but Rodriquez too, currently rent separate storage units there.

On March 10, Rhoades executed a district court approved search warrant for storage units 333, belonging to Rodriquez, and 354, which was Bryant's.

Several publications depicting child pornography were seized from Bryant's unit 354.

During the search on Rodriquez's storage unit 333, the agent found and seized the following books:

Handjobs, Barbarian Chronicles I—the Legacy of Slava that contained about 100 sexually implicit illustrations of adult males engaged in sexual acts with male adolescents;

Mom, Dad, and Bobby that illustrated on the cover an adult female and male and adolescent male in a sexual pose. The book graphically described incestuous sexual acts between a mother, father and their adolescent son named Bobby.

Slave Boys in Bondage depicting graphically described stories of sexual acts between adult males and adolescent males;

Sister Showed Him How depicting explicit stories of adult males engaged in sexual acts with females ages seven to 11 and of an act of bestiality between a seven-year-old girl and a German shepherd dog;

and Handjobs, Daddy Boy Stories depicting about 13 sexually explicit illustrations of adult males engaged in sexual acts with boys, including one account of a father and juvenile son.

The agent also seized from Rodriquez storage unit in T or C amateur type written stories including stories of a brother and sister touching each others genitalia, an act of bestiality between an adolescent male and Labrador dog, sex acts between two brothers, ages 12 and 14; sex acts between two adolescent brothers and their father, and lastly of incestuous sexual acts between mothers, fathers and adolescent sons, according to Rhoades' statement of facts.

The setting of a preliminary examination in state magistrate court, which will determine whether there is probable cause to bind over the defendant to district court for trial on the felony charge, was pending as of press time Thursday.

James Bryant (far right with glasses) sits among acquaintances in Truth or Consequences several years before he reportedly committed suicide in the wake of a state police investigation that uncovered his appetite for pornographic books and videotapes that exploited children as well as snuff films that were found inside his home. According to Agent Norman Rhoades in court documents he filed, Bryant delved in sexual fantasies involving babies, playing the role with his lover, Anthony Rodriguez of Las Cruces. Questions are yet unanswered as to whether Bryant actually engaged in sexual relations with boys or babies, or whether his activities involved only adults.

Sierra County's first child porn possession case dropped

By Bill Johnson of the Desert Journal
Monday, August 18, 2003

The state has dismissed its first case of child pornography possession in Sierra County because of a lack of evidence, Deputy District Attorney Tim Garner said today.

As such, Anthony Rodriquez, 36, a resident of Las Cruces who was living in Truth or Consequences, will avoid facing justice on a fourth degree felony charge of sexual exploitation of children.

Garner said the dismissal was granted by the Seventh Judicial District Court in T or C a couple of months ago after he requested it.

"After a review of the case, I found that the evidence didn't prove the elements we're required to prove. There were no actual children we could prove were involved in this case," said Garner, whose predecessor, June Stein, originally approved of the charges to be filed.

Garner said a recent U.S. Supreme Court ruling also requires that the state must have live victims that could be identified in child porn possession cases. Writings and photographs must be things that actually happened with a young child before a case is considered valid, Garner said.

"You can't be prosecuted for your own imagination," Garner said.

The case actually began as an offshoot of the David Parker Ray trail of sexual torture case in Elephant Butte nearly four and a half years ago and it focused not on Rodriquez, but on his homosexual lover James Bryant, who reportedly committed suicide earlier this year at his residence in Las Cruces at 1421 Wyoming St.

Supervising Agent Norman Rhoades of the New Mexico State Police Criminal Investigation Section in Las Cruces filed the charge against Rodriquez in March, although the case for the police detective dated back to April 19, 1999, about a month after the infamous case involving David Ray broke.

According to the court briefs Rhoades filed in court, James Bryant had maintained books and videotapes containing child pornography and snuff films inside his residence. The agent also learned Bryant delved in sexual fantasies involving babies, playing the role with his lover Rodriquez.

<<< >>>

David Ray case still an open book

Many loose ends to tie up

By Bill Johnson of the Desert Journal
August 18, 2003

Cindy Hendy again tried to challenge the sentencing passed onto her for her role in the kidnapping, rape and torture of two women in February and March 1999 but the judge recently ordered her to continue serving her 36-year prison term.

Former Assistant District Attorney Jim Yontz intervened on behalf of Hendy during the hearing on the motion to reduce sentencing before District Judge Kevin Sweazea based on the fact she cooperated with police and prosecutors from the start after her arrest in late March 1999. The hearing was held about two weeks ago in the state district court in Truth or Consequences.

Specifically, Yontz told the court that Hendy gave the prosecution two homicides and that she had given more information on major crimes than anyone he ever dealt with—both as a police officer and as a prosecuting attorney.

Sgt. Rich Libicer, supervisor in charge of the New Mexico State Police Criminal Investigation Section in Las Cruces who was in charge of the David Ray investigation at Elephant Butte in 1999, said today that as part of Hendy's plea agreement, she was to provide information to investigators regarding the case. "But she hasn't done that," Libicer said during a phone interview Monday.

Libicer said Hendy, who was David Ray's accomplice and girlfriend, may have thought the information she gave police was valid. "But it was not."

Asked about which homicides Yontz was referring to, Libicer said he didn't know exactly because he wasn't at the hearing.

He said, however, Hendy offered information on the Marie Parker murder case, to which Roy Yancy plead guilty and was sentenced to 20 years in prison. "However, her information didn't pan out that way," Libicer said.

With Judge Sweazea's ruling, Hendy will serve more time in prison than any of the other three defendants in the case, having pled guilty to kidnapping and rape charges. Although David Ray was sentenced to 224 years in prison, he died after serving only three years and his daughter, Jessy Ray, was allowed to go free with time served and with five years of probation. And Hendy's prison term will continue

16 years after Yancy's prison term expires for murdering Parker, a mother of two young children.

Libicer also clarified some of the more controversial points of the case, such as statements that someone other than Yancy killed Parker. He said leads that pointed at Pablo Nuanes, who has never been named a suspect in the Parker murder case, went no where.

Libicer said Yancy confessed to the crime of murdering Parker and that he (Libicer) was there during the police interview with Yancy. Despite what two books and other sources have said about the case, Libicer said that to his knowledge there were no photographs taken of the murder incident at the time it happened and that there were no guns involved in a threat.

Libicer said Yancy stated to police investigators that both Jessy and David Ray were present at the time he strangled Marie Parker to death in Ray's toy box after she had been held there for two days and two nights in captivity.

"There was no gun but there were implied threats. "Yancy said he was afraid of David Ray. His story is David Ray (not Jessy Ray as reported in *Cries in the Desert* by John Glatt) ordered Yancy to kill Marie," the state police agent said.

But Libicer said he's skeptical about Yancy's statement. "I don't think Yancy was afraid of David Ray. What we believe is that Yancy killed Marie Parker."

However, Libicer said police so far haven't been able to prove probable cause that Yancy may have been involved in the homicide of Kenneth Lee Lane, whose body was found Jan. 1, 1996, inside his rock house apartment on West Second Street in Truth or Consequences after neighbors smelled his badly decomposed remains through a wall heater in their adjoining apartment.

At the time T or C City Police ruled Lane's death as a suicide, although Detective Priscilla Torrez at the time told the neighbors she at first thought it was a murder.

Yancy was connected to the case because he, along with Jessy Ray, were Lane's only known visitors and because Yancy had visited Lane four or five days before Lane's body was found in his apartment.

One neighbor said Lane usually accompanied Yancy when Yancy would leave Lane's apartment but not this particular time and that Lane's motorcycle sat still in one spot for days—which was very unusual—until it was discovered he was dead.

Lane's death was ruled to be from metallic poisoning in which nuts and bolts were found in his stomach and a door knob in his rectum. There were also signs of a struggle and injuries, with blood splattered on the walls, according to the neighbors.

"Yancy was questioned in length about Kenneth Lane," Sgt. Libicer said today. "The case has the earmark of homicide rather than suicide," he said.

Evidence during the initial investigation by city police, however, was destroyed and it will be difficult to prove without a confession, which Yancy would not provide, according to Libicer.

Also in speaking about possible homicide connected to the case, Libicer said one of Jessy Ray's acquaintances or friends in Albuquerque, Jill Troia, was reported missing in July 1996, about the time that Jessy Ray moved to Elephant Butte and before she and her father abducted Kelly.

It would be the same month that Jessy Ray provided a guest editorial to the Desert Journal for publication (see at end of book). The article she wrote is about her frustration in getting help for Ziggy the bird that got injured at Elephant Butte Lake.

Libicer said Troia is still missing to this day.

"The entire case (involving both Rays, Yancy and Hendy) is still open," Libicer said. "We still follow up leads when they come in on that case."

Regarding bodies that may have been buried in Elephant Butte Lake in connection with David Ray's part in the case, Libicer said search and rescue divers have made no attempts since their last intensive search in November 2002.

"I was on the diving team for seven years. It's hard to locate a person's body in such a massive body of water," he said.

"A sweep search (in which agents hold a line to sweep an area on the bottom of the lake) is not practical for our team in Elephant Butte Lake. You need a specific area to search," he said.

Regarding the burlap bag of human remains that were found floating on the lake in the wake of the investigation, Libicer said the bag contained just flesh—no meat and no bones.

He said the DNA lab got a DNA profile for the remains. "It was an adult human, probably a female, but we have nothing to compare it to," he said. He said the comparison would be made with other DNA samples that came from, for example, a missing person, but there are none so far.

Apparently the remains don't belong to Marie Parker, whose body has not yet been found although Yancy attempted unsuccessfully to show investigators a burial place in an arroyo or canyon north of T or C and east of the lake after his arrest in April 1999.

Besides the Parker murder, the only other possible homicide that Hendy could have helped police with is that of the unsolved case involving victim Billy Ray Bowers, who was David Ray's boss at Canal Motors in Phoenix, AZ, at the time he ended up missing in the late 1980s, according to Libicer.

A year later the body of a John Doe rose to the surface of Elephant Butte Lake wrapped in blue tarpaulin and with a boat anchor or two. Police found that Bowers had been executed—shot in the back of the head with a bullet—before being dumped in the lake. The body's identity wasn't known until 10 years later and until a week after David Ray's arrest in March 1999.

"The Bowers case is still under investigation," Libicer said. If Ray is found to have been responsible there will be no way to prove it in court of law since he's dead.

Libicer said searches for bodies of possible homicide victims have not been confined to Elephant Butte Lake. "Teams also have checked caves and mine shafts," he said, "but found nothing."

"Eventually, something is going to surface, especially with a case of this magnitude. It's just a matter of time," Agent Libicer said.

Libicer acknowledged some involvement of the occult or occult related crimes (ritualistic and self-styled) in the case, but he said he doesn't believe David Ray could be dubbed a Satanists.

"David Ray used the occult as a measure of control over his victims. He was around weak minded people and used fear to control them," Libicer said.

But Yancy did have a known history of being involved in the occult, despite his brother's denials, as a youth and possibly later as an adult through his associations.

"Yancy was one of those people who David Ray associated with. I'm sure some people around [David Ray] were involved (in the occult or occult related crimes)," Libicer said.

Lastly, Libicer said he has found no signs of dismemberment or snuff films (of rape related murders) from among the thousand pieces of evidence that police seized from Ray's home and toy box—where the sign that read "Satan's Den" hung—more than four years ago.

Who shall help our injured wildlife when animal protection agency won't [1]

Guest Editorial by Glenda [Jessy] Ray of Elephant Butte
July 19, 1996

On Saturday, July 6, I took possession of a wild waterfowl from Elephant Butte State Park employee Larry Luna. The bird obviously had been caught in a line and a fisherman had severed her left leg to save it—his line, that is.

Unfortunately, this is a common occurrence in the water areas of New Mexico. Besides being a little indignant and aggravated, the bird was quite healthy. Now keeping wildlife, even helping, can have legal implications, but I am an ex-veterinarian assistant and used to do volunteer services for a wildlife protection group in Louisiana.

The thing to do was to find the bird, now named Ziggy, medical treatment and a home. As I said, Ziggy was a waterfowl, which limits her to the water. To fly, she has to run on the water, and to dive for food and navigate with speed, two legs are needed. Ziggy was going to be permanently handicapped.

I proceeded to call a variety of Vets in Las Cruces. I finally contacted a Vet who in turn said that they did donate some of their time to wildlife. This was at the Jornada Veterinary Clinic. The Vet who I spoke with gave me a number to a representative of the Sangre de Cristo Wildlife Protection Agency, to find Ziggy a home. I called and received a list of numbers from an answering machine to use in case this person was not at home.

After several more calls, I contacted another representative of Sangre de Cristo WLPA. This person did not want to be named. The unnamed person explained that Sangre de Cristo WLPA reps might be able to give Ziggy a home for 90 days, but if she wasn't able to leave on her own by then, they would have to kill her.

So, I decided to look elsewhere for a home. I contacted the Albuquerque Zoo and they said that they could not keep a handicapped

---

[1] Editor's Note—This editorial by "Jessy" Ray appeared in the Desert Journal at about the same time Jessy abducted Kelly for her father's sadistic sexual pleasures and after she moved to Elephant Butte from Albuquerque, where a close acquaintance or friend of hers, Jill Troia, was reported missing in July 1996 and is still missing to this day, said Sgt. Rich Libicer, supervisor of the New Mexico State Police Criminal Investigation Section in Las Cruces, who was in charge of the Elephant Butte investigation in 1999.

bird at the zoo, but they did have individuals to contact who would find a permanent home for Ziggy for the rest of her natural lifespan. That problem was taken care of. I couldn't take Ziggy to Las Cruces until Monday.

Larry Luna bought two dozen minnows and Ziggy ate 13 as she was swimming around in my bathtub. She ate five more minnows Monday morning. She was healthy and very alert before and after I arrived at the Vet's office Monday. After waiting about 45 minutes, the Vet., D. Colista, was able to see us. Dr. Colista noted how calm and alert Ziggy was, and also that there was no infection in her left leg. I had been treating it with a local antiseptic- anesthetic.

Dr. Colista also told me that the surgery would be no problem, and said I could call at noon the next day to find out when to pick her up. Before I left, I explained explicitly how to care for the bird and her particular problems with her disability.

When I arrived home, my father (also a State Parks employee) informed me that a woman from Sangre de Cristo WLPA had called and said that Dr. Colista really did not want to do the surgery because it was a difficult procedure. The woman who called also wanted to make sure that the bird was going to have a home.

My father verified all of this. Monday at noon I called to check on Ziggy and at that time I was told that Jerry Tillet, a Sangre de Cristo WLPA rep, went to Dr. Colista's office and noticed that Ziggy was a common Grebe rather than its cousin—the not so common Lon, so decided that no one would want it and told the Vet to kill it.

No one contacted me, I had to call them to find out this information. Of course, when the receptionist informed me of this I was quite shocked. She then gave me Jerry Tillet's number.

Now it was a race to save Ziggy before the Vet put her down. I called Tillet's number and left a message for her to contact me immediately concerning Ziggy. I waited diligently by the phone for about one hour hoping that the Vet would be detained. Jerry Tillet finally contacted me. She explained that because it wasn't an uncommon bird, and it was handicapped, that basically their service didn't consider it important enough to save and didn't think the Albuquerque Zoo would either.

I explained about the Friends of the Zoo and also informed her of all the people involved, unofficially, of course. Game and Fish Department officials also had been contacted and agreed to my course of action. Tillet then offered to call Dr. Colista to make sure that Ziggy was alive and to ask him to go ahead with surgery.

She called me back a few minutes later and said that Ziggy was fine, also asking about transportation after surgery. I informed her that a military police officer from White Sands would transport the bird from Las Cruces to Elephant Butte. She said that would be fine and that she would call back when Ziggy was ready to go.

A few hours later Tillet called to inform me that Ziggy was dead. Ziggy did not go in for surgery at all. I just couldn't understand how a large healthy bird with no infection in her wound, and plenty of anger in her blood for the injustice, could suddenly sicken and die within a few hours, without a little help.

The Sangre de Cristo Wildlife Protection Agency explained that common species in the area were not considered as important as the more rare species from out of state.

If our own local wildlife protection agencies don't care for our indigenous wildlife, then who will? Perhaps one day the common Grebe won't be so common anymore.

Anyway, so much for the Sangre de Cristo Wildlife Protection Agency.

<<< >>>

A Year in Hell

By Deanna Conley
June 30, 2004

I dated Dennis Roy Yancy from March 1992 to June 1993 — one year and three months. It took me that long to realize that the relationship was over.

It took me two years after it was over to admit that I had been in an abusive relationship. It took me even longer than that to admit that it was not my fault.

Eleven years is a long time to harbor feelings of resentment, guilt and suspicion, and I have been told by more than one person to "just forget it."

But how do you forget a year of mind games, hurt, betrayal and incidents of physical confrontation? How do you forget that you stayed in one place and accepted it all?

The thing about the abuse; the thing many people don't understand, is that I adamantly stated that I would never be in that position but by the time I was ready to admit that I was in that position I felt it was too late to retreat.

An abuser rarely hits on the first date. The first few months of dating Roy were excellent. I had previous boyfriends but felt that Roy was "the one" and I was in relationship bliss.

Suffering from low self-esteem that stemmed from elementary school and beyond, I was in disbelief that a man as handsome, charming, witty and popular as Roy was interested in me. Of course, I had been living in New Mexico for only a year at that time so I did not know him in high school and the people that he introduced me to were all friends and all seemed to adore him as much as I did.

I knew nothing of the rumors of Satanic Rites although I had heard stories but never in connection with him. He had even told me of the burglary of a teacher's home but he had said it was a stupid prank and they later made amends for it to the teacher.

Before I moved to New Mexico my grandma had told me a story along the similar lines, but exaggerated by gossip I had assumed at the time, and an added tale of a small dog that had been killed in what was assumed to be for Satanic reasons. Those stories were stored in my memory but by the time I started dating Roy those memories were slightly dusty and cobwebbed and I never made the connection that they were about the man I was dating.

All I knew was that I was in love and I never wanted it to end. The fights were gradual and after each one there were apologies (usually made by me) and promises that we'd never fight again. Each time I believed in the promises made and I knew in my heart and soul that if I were just a better person then I wouldn't make him so mad.

But even though I tried to be all the things he wanted me to be there was always something new. There was a time when he assumed I was cheating on him (just to ease curiosities, I had the chance once and turned it down because I didn't want to hurt Roy that way. There's an irony to be found in this later) and he counted the condom packs in our nightstand drawer. I have no idea how many were in there before, I was not in the habit of counting them each day, and I'm sure he didn't either; however, he just "knew" that two of the packs were gone.

He hunted all over the house looking for used condoms or empty packs. When he didn't find any he shoved his hands down my pants to see if I was "wet." Apparently that satisfied him because he apologized and said that maybe he was wrong about the count.

How does a person fight insanity like that? But still, I did not waver in my belief that to change the cycle of abuse I had to change myself since I was the "cause" of it.

Looking back now I can see that a lot of fights were caused by some inane idea that surfaced in his sick mind. A lot of them really were my fault but only in the way that I stood up for myself. It might seem hard to believe because if I truly had stood up for myself I would have left or called the police, or at least asked someone to help me.

But, if I had been the compliant and subservient woman he seemed to want then maybe we wouldn't have fought at all… I don't really believe that, not anymore anyway.

But I did stand up for myself on certain issues. When he wanted me to no longer see my friends I stood up for myself. I lost and had to see my friends sneakily, but I did stand up for myself. I argued back and when he pushed me around I pushed back. No one seems to understand that I did fight, I fought for my life and tried to fight for me… for the person I was before I met him.

Yeah, I am to blame for some of the fights but he deserved every one of them. The times that were tough were the situations I had no control over, such as with the condoms. When those inane ideas came to surface there was no telling what could happen.

We had a joint checking account at one time and he was not very good about logging checks or ATM withdrawals into the registry. He went out one night with a male friend and two female friends. He stopped by the ATM to get alcohol money and the ATM told him "insufficient funds."

We were living on his parents' property at the time in Palomas Circle. We had one of those truck bed campers — the kind with the bunk bed that extends over the top of the cab of the truck. It was secured down and served as our bedroom.

I was inside probably writing poetry and drinking to avoid the emotional pain I was feeling and trying not to think of what he was doing with the girls. I heard the car pull up and knew that he was furious about something by the way that the brakes squealed, and through the window I could see the dust rise up.

Roy used to keep a metal baseball bat inside his car and he came flying out of the car swinging that bat. He was convinced that I had pulled all of our money out of the bank. He never stopped to think that we only had one ATM card and he had kept it all day.

I heard the bat hit the ground and all I could do was sit and wonder how much it was going to hurt when he finally made it inside. I had locked the door as soon as he jumped out of the car but the window in the door was Plexiglas and big enough that once broken he reached inside and unlocked the door.

I never knew if his fist or his the bat broke the window but I knew that when I saw his hand unlock the door that I wouldn't have to wonder for long what it would feel like to be hit with a metal bat.

Fortunately for me he must have spent his rage on the ground because I still do not know what it is like to be hit with a metal bat. I reminded him that he had possessed the card all day; I reminded him that we were never very good about balancing our checkbook. And I probably gave him whatever money I had on me and he left again.

The next day we went down to the bank and had them balance our checkbook. The proof was right there that I had not pulled any money out that day. After we left he apologized and said I was right. He always apologized and would admit if I was right and he was wrong.

But what he never did was admit that he had ever hit or threatened me. To this day I doubt he will ever admit it.

I say this because almost two years after we were broke up for good I was in Truth or Consequences (I had previously lived in Las Cruces). I saw Roy at Pixie's discount store. He knew that I had been engaged and heard that it had ended. He gives me a big hug as if we were long-time friends and said, "I don't know why guys keep treating you that way."

Whether he included himself on that list I'll never know. But I do know that he thought we were friends because he constantly asked my family for my address.

After that failed engagement I went back to Cruces to finish my education at New Mexico State University and I purposely lost all connections with mutual friends of Roy's and mine. I told my family that if they gave out my address, and later my married name, I would never speak to them again and move again without giving them the new address.

My family is very close and loving and no one betrayed me. My brother would get annoyed with it and tell Roy that I lived in a house — in New Mexico, in the U.S., on the planet Earth. My grandmother told him to "go to hell."

Everyone else just ignored him. My friends in Cruces thought I was paranoid. But five years after I had last seen Roy that day in Pixie's he was arrested for the murder of Marie Parker. Two weeks before that he had asked my brother for my address.

I knew Marie briefly. Roy cheated on me with her. When we were broke up for the final time we had been on a bowling league for the summer for mixed couples.

The bowling alley was called Pleasure Center then and somehow I was convinced to still bowl the last game even though the thought of seeing Roy and not being his girl was heart breaking. Marie was there. She took me aside and asked me two things.

One of those things I will regret forever and the other I do not regret. Marie asked me if I wanted her to leave. She said she realized that I must be uncomfortable and since I was bowling I had to be there, but she didn't.

Because she took the high road I took it too and told her that as the new girlfriend she had just as much right to be there. I do not regret that. I think that moment made me strong and I don't regret it.

What I do regret is that she asked me if Roy was abusive because she had heard rumors. It took me two years to admit it to myself, there was no way I could admit it after only two weeks and to a woman I didn't even know and who essentially "stole" him from me. I told her "no."

She said that as his girlfriend she figured I would know better than anyone and as a woman she trusted me.

Everyone tells me her murder was not my fault and I could not have prevented it. Part of me accepts that but another part of me knows that if I had told her things maybe she wouldn't have been so trusting.

Maybe she saw his evil side, maybe she saw it and was still trusting as I was so many times. I didn't keep my address from him for fear of him hurting me. I certainly didn't fear the "Toy Box" because no one knew about it at the time.

I kept my address from him because I was afraid of being charmed by him once again and letting him back in my life. To this day that is still my greatest fear. Even though I am thousands of miles from him I still worry that one day he will call or show up on my doorstep. And I worry even more that I will accept him.

But back to Marie. I feel that if I had told her things then maybe the story would be different. Told her about the baseball bat. Told her about the time he pointed a 9 mm at my head with the bizarre idea a murder-suicide was the only way to stop fighting.

If I had told her that he mentioned to me once he wanted to kill someone just to see what it would feel like. If I had told her that he had strangled me then maybe she would have been less trusting. If I had told the police about it maybe he would have been incarcerated before he had a chance to kill Marie.

There are a lot of maybes and a lot of questions for which there will never be an answer. All I know for certain is that I regret lying to her. I regretted it 10 seconds after I did it and I exonerated myself by promising that I would apologize and explain it all to her one day.

When my brother said that he was interested in dating Marie I hoped my exoneration was close at hand. She was with my brother the night she left the bar and disappeared. My ex-boyfriend killed the woman my brother wanted to date. That's something to try living with!

I have to live with all these memories and the slightest thing can trigger it. If a man raises his hand too quickly I flinch. I cannot stand the sight of guns, even toy guns, or the sounds that they make.

Roy had a BB gun that I bought him during the time we had gone to Wisconsin and stayed with one of my brothers. He used to shoot it in the house all the time. He shot it out the window once and aimed it at one of the neighbor kids. From the third story apartment window down to the parking lot it still packed a good wallop and hit a four-year-old boy in the back.

The police came to talk to us as they talked to all the tenants, but their suspicions were on Roy because the other kids saw him lean out the window at the time, although none claimed to have seen a gun. I had seen the police coming and we tried to hide the targets Roy shot at and moved posters around to cover up BB holes.

I know the police didn't believe us because I saw one of them look at the wall and I knew he had seen the BB marks. The whole time that I lied to the cops I was thinking, "End it now. Tell them he shot the boy and tell them everything else."

But Roy and I and a friend with us at the time all lied to the cops. They told us the BB had hit a quarter of an inch away from his spine. They said the quarter inch was the only thing that saved the boy from paralysis.

I don't know if a BB can cause paralysis on a four-year-old boy. But I know that Roy should have been cuffed and hauled away a long time before he murdered Marie.

My husband bought a BB gun a few years into our marriage. Every time he brought it out to target practice outside I flinched. He doesn't bring it out anymore when I am around.

I also cannot tolerate anyone's hands or arms around my neck, even in a light and affectionate manner. I cannot recall what the fight was about at that point but I remember being pinned down by Roy.

I don't even remember his hands ever moving to my throat — my memory starts with being strangled and spots appearing in my vision. Roy was infatuated with AC/DC, a hard metal rock band, and felt as if they wrote songs simply for him. AC/DC was one thing that you did not mess with around Roy. He was wearing a white AC/DC concert T-shirt at the time.

The only thing I could think of doing was tear at his throat. I grabbed the collar of his shirt and pulled down. It tore about two inches down before he stopped.

He looked at the shirt and looked at me. I knew then that I would die over an AC/DC shirt. But, fortunately it snapped him out of his reverie and he got off of me. The next morning found me sewing an AC/DC shirt and trying to make amends for ruining it.

When people questioned about the stitches he told them it was wild sex and I couldn't wait to get his clothes off. Come to think of it, I think he told his parents something similar about the broken Plexiglas — wild sex and an elbow or knee went through.

The other time that bears mentioning is an incident involving his eyes. In the first edition of "Satan's Den Exposed", I read an account of a woman who was with him and raped. She described his eyes and even though I got chills reading it — and I am sorry that she has to suffer with those memories — I was glad someone witnessed what I did.

Roy was fond of pinning me down with his knees on my shoulders. He had me this way once and was not actually doing anything to me. Nonetheless, I was terrified.

His eyes are green and very hypnotic. To me they always looked like fresh olive slices. However, this time I will swear for the rest of my life that they were white. His eyes looked as if the color had been bleached out of them. The only color that remained was a very thin ring of green around the outer rim of his irises.

I associated that thin layer with his sanity. When that color faded as well I knew that he'd be completely insane.

Roy harbored a fear of going blind so I raked my hands across his eyes. I have always had natural long nails and even though I drew no blood I did leave red welts down his eyes and his cheeks. The next few moments found us with him cowering by the bed whimpering and crying that he had gone blind and I apologizing to him.

To this day I have never seen anything as scary as his eyes were that night and I wish I had scratched harder. Permanent scars over his eyes would be a fitting reminder to him and warning to others. But each event usually left one of us apologizing with amends trying to be made.

Bruises were explained in the same way or to my being a klutz (which is true and anyone who knew me back then knew it so no one really questioned it). I was never hospitalized and never had a serious injury. It is very hard to prove the abuse I went through, even to myself.

It's been so long now that I wonder if my memories play me false. Sometimes I feel like it never happened at all.

There were people who saw the fights and there were people who suspected the fights led to the bruises or threats against my life.

Back then I would not allow anyone to help me. I excused every thing and admitted nothing.

But now? Now I wonder why no one spoke up when New Mexico was bursting with the news of his arrest. In the newspapers he was quoted as being a "nice guy" and he was a T-ball coach for many children. He was. There is no question that he was good. Literally he would give you the shirt off his back. But there was an evil side in there as well.

When the story was headline news why didn't anyone remember or speak up about the evil side? Why didn't one person say, "I remember a fight I saw him in with this one girl." Our fights were often public domain.

Am I the only one to remember his evil side or was I the only one to see it? My family never saw it, but as I said, I hid it well. However, after the news came out my family said how lucky I was that I did keep my address hidden. Luck had nothing to do with it. It was knowledge.

Sure, I was afraid of him charming his way back into my life but I'd be an idiot if I didn't admit that I feared his evil side as well. They will ask me "Did you ever have any idea he could do something like that?" I told them, "Yes." But when I try to tell them what happened the subject always gets conveniently changed. Or if I bring it up at a later date they act as if they don't remember.

This ignorance of what happened to me makes me want to believe that I am wrong. That maybe it was all a bad dream. But the memories are too clear and too sharp for me to honestly accept that.

What I want most of all in this world is for someone who saw things back then to stand up and say they remember. If I could get Roy to stand up and admit it I think I might find some peace.

I'm hoping that this story will help me achieve peace. I can't go on for the rest of my life pretending it didn't happen and harboring guilt for things I should have done or said.

I don't tell this story because I am a bitter ex-girlfriend. I tell this story because no one else can, or won't. I tell this story because it is mine to tell.

Shocking Afterthoughts

I have my own self-critique I'd like to share before finally closing this book. Some people think I'm radical in my approach. But to them I say the truth, when it should be told but most often is not, is sometimes like explosive atoms inside our brain cells. Radical energy just spins and spins and wipes out everything in its path, its bright light exposes our own inner feelings, our most secure thoughts to the rest of the world.

But the truth be known, which I never let known before, is that I hide well the secrets that must be kept locked, not as an evil doer, but as an evil receiver, not to protect my transgressors but to forever give them license to prey upon others among the weak.

Yes, I'm guilty of allowing the guilty to go free because it wouldn't be until 20 years later or during the David Parker Ray & All case that I would remember the eerie events of crimes that happened to me in 1980 in San Francisco, California. Being naïve, I would have no idea that a best friend could dine you, drug you without your knowledge, then rape and disgrace you without you batting an eye because you were out cold.

But one day, 20 years later you wake up screaming in your mind and suddenly recall the events of a five second relapse in your drug induced state, you're struggling and you yell, "No, Stop, Quit" or whatever, and fall unconscious again, not to wake for another 12 hours, maybe a day, who knows, a week…

You trusted that person but they betrayed your trust and violated you and because of it you can't tell anyone because 1) no one will think you're credible; or 2) they'll just think you're betraying your friend with a lie.

So, to the rape victims who are afraid to tell the truth, I dare you to not do what I do and that is to keep the truth inside, locked forever, to haunt you that someone else down the line will fall victim to your transgressors who violated you, and will continue to violate others if you do nothing to stop them.

And if my own transgressor is still out there, Mr. Tom Crowe, the Canadian who fooled Colorado residents to vote for you for state representative in the 1970s, and later in the early 1980s committed rape against me in San Francisco, who shattered my vision of what true friends are—I say to you this:

I hope through the years you never victimized anyone else and I hope you have repented of your sins and that God forgave you. I might even be able to forgive you, but I may never forgive myself for any crimes you may have committed against anyone else after me because I did nothing to stop you. But I have only my memory—which you shattered with your secret pill or whatever it is you did to make me pass out suddenly in your motel room where you lived.

Let's refresh our memories. If I recall correctly, I had just gotten out of a VISTA related meeting around 7 p.m. on an unusually warm October evening in 1980—about a month after I arrived from New Mexico to become a VISTA in San Francisco—and I went to your room, I believe it was at the Ambassador in the Tenderloin District where I also lived for a couple of months. At the time I thought you were some kind of community activist wanting to improve the quality of life in the community, so I became your friend.

We decided to grab a beer at the local pub around the corner and while I went to the restroom you sneakily put some damned pill or powder in my drink because ten minutes after I drank just one beer, I started to get really tired and groggy and we agreed to leave the bar and return to your room for what I thought would be a friendly chat.

A chat turned short and I was out cold. But sometime during the night, in the middle of captivity, your 40-year-old or so big fat blob of a body was on top of mine—then only 150 pounds and a "young chicken" as your predatory lips might say it. I could feel your crushing weight suffocating my puny body then as I lay on your bed—you, a trusted friend violated me.

I said or yelled, "No, No, No" and struggled with what little strength I had under a drug-induced state, but you continued to rape me and the next thing I'm out cold again and the early evening became late morning and for some reason I wake up in your bed. I was a little freaked but I didn't remember the events of that night—not even of the five to ten seconds that I 20 years later would remember of all those horrible things you did to me—never mind while I was unconscious—and how I ached, was sore, felt physically mutilated by the incident and not knowing what happened for a whole 20 years!!!

But for some reason I become tight, I lock up, I become withdrawn, I suffer post traumatic stress disorder, I have a multitude of health problems and I make my family unhappy at times when I get into my mood. No, this book isn't just about the victims of this book—it's all about me too and what I failed to do as a victim, and that was to report Mr. Tom Crowe as my rapist. I hereby submit my complaint and grieve for not remembering sooner the events of that horrible night.

I sob as I write just knowing that you probably never did repent and never did stop your sick behavior of drugging people and raping them—you are a sick, sick person who needs help. But you also should be locked up in prison for your sinister evilness.

Had I stayed awake for more than the five to ten seconds that I awoke to witness my fate with hell, would you have killed me too? Did you tie me up, suspend me from ropes? Take a few photographs or videotapes to get off on later? Have you ever killed anyone? If you have, I can live with that guilt on my conscience too, but remember I'm the victim, I'm the survivor and now you get your swift justice because it has taken me two years, from the day I realized you drugged and raped me, to get brave enough to tell this story. And when I find your photograph I will publish it in a later edition of this book (I know I have a few, it may take me time to find them. The photos are of us at Golden Gate Park at a "company" picnic).

It is the David Parker Ray case that "refreshed" my memory, I say to Mr. Jim Yontz, who insults me twice in *Slow Death* by Jim Fielder. I forgive you. You don't really know me or how I feel, Mr. Yontz. I truly am sorry about your wife, Karen, who worked as an investigator for the attorney general's office, for getting killed in May after the armed bank robbery or after a series of robberies, which she committed in Albuquerque apparently to pay off a gambling debt. I truly am sorry for your lost…

I am sorry I ever gave my photographs and written materials to Mr. John Glatt, author of *Cries in the Desert*, because we never really do get the rewards we should reap from our own hard work, even when there is a contract. (Late entry note—contract terms were satisfied in October 2003).

And to the author of *Slow Death*, Mr. Jim Fielder just steals his material, regardless of how riddled it is with inaccuracies and lies, even when he knows the truth. I suppose it's because of these two books that I decided a third one was needed to tell what is truthful, what is on the public record, or even what is alleged as long as it is followed through with vengeance, to be fair to all so to speak.

I realize the conflicts that arise when you want to get the truth out and of course some issues may never get resolved like whether Jessy Ray, who is free and lives within a few blocks from my house as I write this, had anything to do with the death of Marie Parker. If so, did she and Roy Yancy kidnap Parker, take her to the toy box where Jessy and David Ray then allegedly raped and tortured her two days and nights—as alleged in *Cries in the Desert*, before David Ray allegedly ordered Yancy to kill Marie by strangling her with a rope? I am sorry that you, Jessy Ray, had no comments for me or my reporters at the Desert Journal when we asked you for them because we still don't have your side to the story—not the real side. We don't want the fake one you gave to the TV stations in Albuquerque.

I am also sorry that you, Jessy Ray, have the appearance of a predator and it will take some real persuasion to get me to believe otherwise. But I also realize your good nature, your love for wildlife and the fact you've helped countless people in your time, including my brother-in-law in the repair of his vehicle before he left for Colorado. Some of us truly believe that somehow you're a victim in all of this—at least to the circumstances of having a sick dad—but there seems to be also a dark side to you in which you have kidnapped and delivered young women—or at least one, according to court records—to your father. I hope you have repented and take your freedom seriously, because there are those of us who want to see justice served, especially in the case of Marie Parker's death, and possibly others.

To the rest of the world, I am a victim no more. I probably will escape Truth or Consequences and go into seclusion, hoping my book sells by the millions because my weekly newspaper of nearly eight years failed in May, and my online news service has failed to raise an income since then. My only recourse to financial recovery is this book, which no one can take away. This book is my catharsis, my healing from victimization somewhere deep inside Satan's Den.

/s/Bill Johnson
Editor & Publisher
Desert Journal
www.desertjournalonline.com

August 18, 2003

Tom Crowe (center) with friends at company picnic at Golden Gate Park, San Francisco, October 1980

The Players: Images of the faces throughout this book.

Mugs Collage compiled from DJ file photos

RAMBLE HOUSE's

HARRY STEPHEN KEELER WEBWORK MYSTERIES

(RH) indicates the title is available ONLY in the **RAMBLE HOUSE** edition

The Ace of Spades Murder
The Affair of the Bottled Deuce (RH)
The Amazing Web
The Barking Clock
Behind That Mask
The Book with the Orange Leaves
The Bottle with the Green Wax Seal
The Box from Japan
The Case of the Canny Killer
The Case of the Crazy Corpse (RH)
The Case of the Flying Hands (RH)
The Case of the Ivory Arrow
The Case of the Jeweled Ragpicker
The Case of the Lavender Gripsack
The Case of the Mysterious Moll
The Case of the 16 Beans
The Case of the Transparent Nude (RH)
The Case of the Transposed Legs
The Case of the Two-Headed Idiot (RH)
The Case of the Two Strange Ladies
The Circus Stealers (RH)
Cleopatra's Tears
A Copy of Beowulf (RH)
The Crimson Cube (RH)
The Face of the Man From Saturn
Find the Clock
The Five Silver Buddhas
The 4th King
The Gallows Waits, My Lord! (RH)
The Green Jade Hand
Finger! Finger!
Hangman's Nights (RH)
I, Chameleon (RH)
I Killed Lincoln at 10:13! (RH)
The Iron Ring
The Man Who Changed His Skin (RH)
The Man with the Crimson Box
The Man with the Magic Eardrums
The Man with the Wooden Spectacles
The Marceau Case
The Matilda Hunter Murder
The Monocled Monster
The Murder of London Lew
The Murdered Mathematician
The Mysterious Card (RH)
The Mysterious Ivory Ball of Wong Shing Li (RH)
The Mystery of the Fiddling Cracksman
The Peacock Fan
The Photo of Lady X (RH)
The Portrait of Jirjohn Cobb
Report on Vanessa Hewstone (RH)
Riddle of the Travelling Skull
Riddle of the Wooden Parrakeet (RH)
The Scarlet Mummy (RH)
The Search for X-Y-Z
The Sharkskin Book
Sing Sing Nights
The Six From Nowhere (RH)
The Skull of the Waltzing Clown
The Spectacles of Mr. Cagliostro
Stand By—London Calling!
The Steeltown Strangler
The Stolen Gravestone (RH)
Strange Journey (RH)
The Strange Will
The Straw Hat Murders (RH)
The Street of 1000 Eyes (RH)
Thieves' Nights
Three Novellos (RH)
The Tiger Snake
The Trap (RH)
Vagabond Nights (Defrauded Yeggman)
Vagabond Nights 2 (10 Hours)
The Vanishing Gold Truck
The Voice of the Seven Sparrows
The Washington Square Enigma
When Thief Meets Thief
The White Circle (RH)
The Wonderful Scheme of Mr. Christopher Thorne
X. Jones—of Scotland Yard
Y. Cheung, Business Detective

Keeler Related Works

A To Izzard: A Harry Stephen Keeler Companion by Fender Tucker — Articles and stories about Harry, by Harry, and in his style. Included is a compleat bibliography.

Wild About Harry: Reviews of Keeler Novels — Edited by Richard Polt & Fender Tucker — 22 reviews of works by Harry Stephen Keeler from *Keeler News.* A perfect introduction to the author.

The Keeler Keyhole Collection: Annotated newsletter rants from Harry Stephen Keeler, edited by Francis M. Nevins. Over 400 pages of incredibly personal Keeleriana.

Fakealoo — Pastiches of the style of Harry Stephen Keeler by selected demented members of the HSK Society. Updated every year with the new winner.

RAMBLE HOUSE's OTHER LOONS

Strands of the Web: Short Stories of Harry Stephen Keeler — Edited and Introduced by Fred Cleaver
The Sam McCain Novels — Ed Gorman's terrific series includes *The Day the Music Died, Wake Up Little Susie* and *Will You Still Love Me Tomorrow?*
A Shot Rang Out — Three decades of reviews from Jon Breen
Blood Moon — The first of the Robert Payne series by Ed Gorman
The Time Armada — Fox B. Holden's 1953 SF gem.
Black River Falls — Suspense from the master, Ed Gorman
Sideslip — 1968 SF masterpiece by Ted White and Dave Van Arnam
The Triune Man — Mindscrambling science fiction from Richard A. Lupoff
Detective Duff Unravels It — Episodic mysteries by Harvey O'Higgins
Mysterious Martin, the Master of Murder — Two versions of a strange 1912 novel by Tod Robbins about a man who writes books that can kill.
The Master of Mysteries — 1912 novel of supernatural sleuthing by Gelett Burgess
Dago Red — 22 tales of dark suspense by Bill Pronzini
The Night Remembers — A 1991 Jack Walsh mystery from Ed Gorman
Rough Cut & New, Improved Murder — Ed Gorman's first two novels
Hollywood Dreams — A novel of the Depression by Richard O'Brien
Six Gelett Burgess Novels — *The Master of Mysteries, The White Cat, Two O'Clock Courage, Ladies in Boxes, Find the Woman, The Heart Line*
The Organ Reader — A huge compilation of just about everything published in the 1971-1972 radical bay-area newspaper, *THE ORGAN*.
A Clear Path to Cross — Sharon Knowles short mystery stories by Ed Lynskey
Old Times' Sake — Short stories by James Reasoner from Mike Shayne Magazine
Freaks and Fantasies — Eerie tales by Tod Robbins, collaborator of Tod Browning on the film FREAKS.
Five Jim Harmon Sleaze Double Novels — *Vixen Hollow/Celluloid Scandal, The Man Who Made Maniacs/Silent Siren, Ape Rape/Wanton Witch, Sex Burns Like Fire/Twist Session*, and *Sudden Lust/Passion Strip.* More doubles to come!
Marblehead: A Novel of H.P. Lovecraft — A long-lost masterpiece from Richard A. Lupoff. Published for the first time!
The Compleat Ova Hamlet — Parodies of SF authors by Richard A. Lupoff - New edition!
The Secret Adventures of Sherlock Holmes — Three Sherlockian pastiches by the Brooklyn author/publisher, Gary Lovisi.
The Universal Holmes — Richard A. Lupoff's 2007 collection of five Holmesian pastiches and a recipe for giant rat stew.
Four Joel Townsley Rogers Novels — By the author of *The Red Right Hand: Once In a Red Moon, Lady With the Dice, The Stopped Clock, Never Leave My Bed*
Two Joel Townsley Rogers Story Collections — Night of Horror and Killing Time
Twenty Norman Berrow Novels — *The Bishop's Sword, Ghost House, Don't Go Out After Dark, Claws of the Cougar, The Smokers of Hashish, The Secret Dancer, Don't Jump Mr. Boland!, The Footprints of Satan, Fingers for Ransom, The Three Tiers of Fantasy, The Spaniard's Thumb, The Eleventh Plague, Words Have Wings, One Thrilling Night, The Lady's in Danger, It Howls at Night, The Terror in the Fog, Oil Under the Window, Murder in the Melody, The Singing Room*
The N. R. De Mexico Novels — Robert Bragg presents *Marijuana Girl, Madman on a Drum, Private Chauffeur* in one volume.
Four Chelsea Quinn Yarbro Novels featuring Charlie Moon — *Ogilvie, Tallant and Moon, Music When the Sweet Voice Dies, Poisonous Fruit* and *Dead Mice*
Four Walter S. Masterman Mysteries — *The Green Toad, The Flying Beast, The Yellow Mistletoe* and *The Wrong Verdict,* fantastic impossible plots. More to come.
Two Hake Talbot Novels — *Rim of the Pit, The Hangman's Handyman.* Classic locked room mysteries.
Two Alexander Laing Novels — *The Motives of Nicholas Holtz* and *Dr. Scarlett*, stories of medical mayhem and intrigue from the 30s.
Four David Hume Novels — *Corpses Never Argue, Cemetery First Stop, Make Way for the Mourners, Eternity Here I Come*, and more to come.
Three Wade Wright Novels — *Echo of Fear, Death At Nostalgia Street* and *It Leads to Murder*, with more to come!
Five Rupert Penny Novels — *Policeman's Holiday, Policeman's Evidence, Lucky Policeman, Sealed Room Murder* and *Sweet Poison,* classic impossible mysteries.

Five Jack Mann Novels — Strange murder in the English countryside. *Gees' First Case, Nightmare Farm, Grey Shapes, The Ninth Life, The Glass Too Many.*

Seven Max Afford Novels — *Owl of Darkness, Death's Mannikins, Blood on His Hands, The Dead Are Blind, The Sheep and the Wolves, Sinners in Paradise* and *Two Locked Room Mysteries and a Ripping Yarn* by one of Australia's finest novelists.

Five Joseph Shallit Novels — *The Case of the Billion Dollar Body, Lady Don't Die on My Doorstep, Kiss the Killer, Yell Bloody Murder, Take Your Last Look.* One of America's best 50's authors.

Two Crimson Clown Novels — By Johnston McCulley, author of the Zorro novels, *The Crimson Clown* and *The Crimson Clown Again.*

The Best of 10-Story Book — edited by Chris Mikul, over 35 stories from the literary magazine Harry Stephen Keeler edited.

A Young Man's Heart — A forgotten early classic by Cornell Woolrich

The Anthony Boucher Chronicles — edited by Francis M. Nevins
Book reviews by Anthony Boucher written for the *San Francisco Chronicle,* 1942 - 1947. Essential and fascinating reading.

Muddled Mind: Complete Works of Ed Wood, Jr. — David Hayes and Hayden Davis deconstruct the life and works of a mad genius.

Gadsby — A lipogram (a novel without the letter E). Ernest Vincent Wright's last work, published in 1939 right before his death.

My First Time: The One Experience You Never Forget — Michael Birchwood — 64 true first-person narratives of how they lost it.

Automaton — Brilliant treatise on robotics: 1928-style! By H. Stafford Hatfield

The Incredible Adventures of Rowland Hern — Rousing 1928 impossible crimes by Nicholas Olde.

Slammer Days — Two full-length prison memoirs: *Men into Beasts* (1952) by George Sylvester Viereck and *Home Away From Home* (1962) by Jack Woodford

Murder in Black and White — 1931 classic tennis whodunit by Evelyn Elder

Killer's Caress — Cary Moran's 1936 hardboiled thriller

The Golden Dagger — 1951 Scotland Yard yarn by E. R. Punshon

Beat Books #1 — Two beatnik classics, *A Sea of Thighs* by Ray Kainen and *Village Hipster* by J.X. Williams

A Smell of Smoke — 1951 English countryside thriller by Miles Burton

Ruled By Radio — 1925 futuristic novel by Robert L. Hadfield & Frank E. Farncombe

Murder in Silk — A 1937 Yellow Peril novel of the silk trade by Ralph Trevor

The Case of the Withered Hand — 1936 potboiler by John G. Brandon

Finger-prints Never Lie — A 1939 classic detective novel by John G. Brandon

Inclination to Murder — 1966 thriller by New Zealand's Harriet Hunter

Invaders from the Dark — Classic werewolf tale from Greye La Spina

Fatal Accident — Murder by automobile, a 1936 mystery by Cecil M. Wills

The Devil Drives — A prison and lost treasure novel by Virgil Markham

Dr. Odin — Douglas Newton's 1933 potboiler comes back to life.

The Chinese Jar Mystery — Murder in the manor by John Stephen Strange, 1934

The Julius Caesar Murder Case — A classic 1935 re-telling of the assassination by Wallace Irwin that's much more fun than the Shakespeare version

West Texas War and Other Western Stories — by Gary Lovisi

The Contested Earth and Other SF Stories — A never-before published space opera and seven short stories by Jim Harmon.

Tales of the Macabre and Ordinary — Modern twisted horror by Chris Mikul, author of the *Bizarrism* series.

The Gold Star Line — Seaboard adventure from L.T. Reade and Robert Eustace.

The Werewolf vs the Vampire Woman — Hard to believe ultraviolence by either Arthur M. Scarm or Arthur M. Scram.

Black Hogan Strikes Again — Australia's Peter Renwick pens a tale of the outback.

Don Diablo: Book of a Lost Film — Two-volume treatment of a western by Paul Landres, with diagrams. Intro by Francis M. Nevins.

The Charlie Chaplin Murder Mystery — Movie hijinks by Wes D. Gehring

The Koky Comics — A collection of all of the 1978-1981 Sunday and daily comic strips by Richard O'Brien and Mort Gerberg, in two volumes.

Suzy — Another collection of comic strips from Richard O'Brien and Bob Vojtko

Dime Novels: Ramble House's 10-Cent Books — *Knife in the Dark* by Robert Leslie Bellem, *Hot Lead* and *Song of Death* by Ed Earl Repp, *A Hashish House in New York* by H.H. Kane, and five more.

Blood in a Snap — The *Finnegan's Wake* of the 21st century, by Jim Weiler and Al Gorithm

Stakeout on Millennium Drive — Award-winning Indianapolis Noir — Ian Woollen.

Dope Tales #1 — Two dope-riddled classics; *Dope Runners* by Gerald Grantham and *Death Takes the Joystick* by Phillip Condé.

Dope Tales #2 — Two more narco-classics; *The Invisible Hand* by Rex Dark and *The Smokers of Hashish* by Norman Berrow.

Dope Tales #3 — Two enchanting novels of opium by the master, Sax Rohmer. *Dope* and *The Yellow Claw.*

Tenebrae — Ernest G. Henham's 1898 horror tale brought back.

The Singular Problem of the Stygian House-Boat — Two classic tales by John Kendrick Bangs about the denizens of Hades.

Tiresias — Psychotic modern horror novel by Jonathan M. Sweet.

The One After Snelling — Kickass modern noir from Richard O'Brien.

The Sign of the Scorpion — 1935 Edmund Snell tale of oriental evil.

The House of the Vampire — 1907 poetic thriller by George S. Viereck.

An Angel in the Street — Modern hardboiled noir by Peter Genovese.

The Devil's Mistress — Scottish gothic tale by J. W. Brodie-Innes.

The Lord of Terror — 1925 mystery with master-criminal, Fantômas.

The Lady of the Terraces — 1925 adventure by E. Charles Vivian.

My Deadly Angel — 1955 Cold War drama by John Chelton

Prose Bowl — Futuristic satire — Bill Pronzini & Barry N. Malzberg .

Satan's Den Exposed — True crime in Truth or Consequences New Mexico — Award-winning journalism by the *Desert Journal*.

The Amorous Intrigues & Adventures of Aaron Burr — by Anonymous — Hot historical action.

I Stole $16,000,000 — A true story by cracksman Herbert E. Wilson.

The Black Dark Murders — Vintage 50s college murder yarn by Milt Ozaki, writing as Robert O. Saber.

Sex Slave — Potboiler of lust in the days of Cleopatra — Dion Leclerq.

You'll Die Laughing — Bruce Elliott's 1945 novel of murder at a practical joker's English countryside manor.

The Private Journal & Diary of John H. Surratt — The memoirs of the man who conspired to assassinate President Lincoln.

Dead Man Talks Too Much — Hollywood boozer by Weed Dickenson

Red Light — History of legal prostitution in Shreveport Louisiana by Eric Brock. Includes wonderful photos of the houses and the ladies.

A Snark Selection — Lewis Carroll's *The Hunting of the Snark* with two Snarkian chapters by Harry Stephen Keeler — Illustrated by Gavin L. O'Keefe.

Ripped from the Headlines! — The Jack the Ripper story as told in the newspaper articles in the *New York* and *London Times.*

Geronimo — S. M. Barrett's 1905 autobiography of a noble American.

The White Peril in the Far East — Sidney Lewis Gulick's 1905 indictment of the West and assurance that Japan would never attack the U.S.

The Compleat Calhoon — All of Fender Tucker's works: Includes *The Totah Trilogy, Weed, Women and Song* and *Tales from the Tower,* plus a CD of all of his songs.

RAMBLE HOUSE

Fender Tucker, Prop.

www.ramblehouse.com fender@ramblehouse.com

228-826-1783 10329 Sheephead Drive, Vancleave MS 39565

www.ingramcontent.com/pod-product-compliance
Lightning Source LLC
LaVergne TN
LVHW050641100826
845148LV00011B/1940

* 9 7 8 1 6 0 5 4 3 0 8 7 4 *